Isaac Myer

Presidential power over Personal liberty

A Review of Horace Binney's essay on the writ of habeas corpus

Isaac Myer

Presidential power over Personal liberty
A Review of Horace Binney's essay on the writ of habeas corpus

ISBN/EAN: 9783337041625

Printed in Europe, USA, Canada, Australia, Japan

Cover: Foto ©ninafisch / pixelio.de

More available books at **www.hansebooks.com**

PRESIDENTIAL POWER

OVER

PERSONAL LIBERTY.

A

REVIEW

OF

HORACE BINNEY'S

ESSAY ON THE

𝔚rit of 𝔥abeas ℭorpus.

IMPRINTED FOR THE AUTHOR.
1862.

ERRATA.

Page 7. 5th line from the top, instead of " we will," read—" will we."

Page 28. 11th line from the top between " be," and " free," strike out " a."

Page 43. 10th line from the bottom, instead of "negatively," read—"negativing."

Page 47. 23d line from the top between "names," and " of," insert, " and works."

Page 66. Last line, for " faithfully," read—" duly."

Page 79. 5th line from the bottom, for " and," read—" or."

INTRODUCTORY.

> "Be just, and fear not:
> Let all the ends thou aim'st at be thy country's,
> Thy God's, and truth's."   II Hen. VIII., Act 3.

THE writer of the following pages, in presenting them to the favorable consideration of the reader, would say that he is not governed by any motives but those which exist within the breast of a sincere lover of his country, nurtured in the belief that a Republican Government is the best devised for the benefit of mankind, individually or in the concrete, as regards their present welfare and future advancement; and that the danger to be feared and avoided, under such a form of government, is centralization—the encroachment of the Executive upon the Legislative or Judicial powers, or all or each upon the rights of the people. He cannot, with such feelings, but believe it to be the duty of every true lover of his country to ward off such a catastrophe; and he has viewed with dread and suspicion endeavors made by learned lawyers to make a precedent of the acts of the Executive relating to arrests and detainer, without the benefit of the Writ of Habeas Corpus, by trying to prove their correctness. If the supporters of the President had been willing that, like General Jackson, he should take the legal responsibility, the writer would have been satisfied, believing that the disease would work its own cure; but, if so great an encroachment upon all the principles of Liberty is to be allowed as legal and right in more ambitious hands, our liberties will fade as a flower, and will always have hanging over them a sword suspended like that of Damocles. The arguments in favor of the right of the Executive to arrest and detain, without the benefit of the Writ, may be found in the North American Review for October, 1861, said to have been written by the Hon. Joel Parker, of the Cambridge Law School; the Opinion of the Attorney General of the United States; and a pamphlet written by Horace Binney, Esq., of Philadelphia. That of the latter is very subtle, and is the best written upon the subject; and as it goes over, to some extent, the arguments of the others—especially as to the meaning of the word *privilege*, in the ninth section of Article I. of the Constitution of the United States, (*vide* N. A. Rev., 490, &c., Opin. of Att'y Gen., 10, &c.,)—to it we shall principally confine our attention. It is very elaborate, and, as far as that side of the question goes, thoroughly exhaustive; and it is advanced with such apparent sincerity that we cannot but surmise that, although it is fallacious, he has reasoned himself into a belief of its correctness.

"We all know," says a great English thinker, "what specious fallacies may be urged in defence of every act of injustice yet proposed for the imaginary benefit of the mass. We know how many, not otherwise fools or bad men, have thought it justifiable to repudiate the national debt. We know how easily the uselessness of almost every branch of knowledge may be proved, to the complete satisfaction of those who do not possess it. How many, not altogether stupid men, think the scientific study of languages useless—think ancient literature useless, all erudition useless, poetry and the fine arts idle and frivolous, political economy purely mischievous. Even history has been pronounced useless and mischievous by able men." (Mill on Gov't, 127.)

An argument founded on opposition to known custom, precedent and history, dangerous to the liberty of the citizen, to the continuation of the Republic, and to the welfare of the social system, should be as clear as the light of that glorious orb which rules the day, and as the blue ether through which comes its golden rays to light the earth.

It will be the endeavor of the writer to give the legal argument, not strained, supported by the authorities he was able to obtain in the short space of time and the limited means at his command. It is also his desire to give an unprejudiced argument; and he will endeavor to be governed by history, reason, and the clear light of that science "which covers with its ashes," to use the words of Finch, "the sparks of all the sciences." The question does not depend upon the law-books alone. Law is obliged to call to her aid History. The conclusion is none the less legal. This conclusion will be, that the Executive has not the power to arrest and detain citizens at his own pleasure, and that the privilege of the Writ of Habeas Corpus cannot be legally or constitutionally suspended without the consent of Congress. There have been no decisions directly in point; though the text writers' and jurists' opinions on the subject are, that Congress must give its consent before a suspension of the privilege can take place. We will, therefore, not be controlled, in this discussion, "by the crooked cord of the discretion" and opinion of Judges found in books of Reports, but "by the golden metwand" of reason, the words of the statute, and cotemporaneous understanding.

We shall consider the subject as follows:—

I. Origin and History of the Writ of Habeas Corpus in England.
    1. Magna Charta.
    2. The Petition of Right.
    3. The Writ of Habeas Corpus.
    4. The Habeas Corpus Act of Charles II.
    5. The Bill of Rights.
    6. Statute of 56th Geo. III., c. 100.
    7. Suspension of the Effect of the Writ in England.

II. Origin and History of the Writ in America.
    1. Magna Charta in America.
    2. Habeas Corpus in America.
    3. Suspension of the Privilege in America.

III. The Privilege of the Writ under the Constitution.
    1. The Right of Arrest by the Executive.
    2. The Right of Suspension of the Privilege and Detainer by the Executive.

THE WRIT OF HABEAS CORPUS.

ITS ORIGIN AND HISTORY IN ENGLAND.

OF great importance to the public is the preservation of this personal liberty; for if once it were left in the power of the highest magistrate to imprison arbitrarily, whomever he or his officers thought proper, there would soon be an end of all other rights and immunities. To bereave a man of life, or by violence to confiscate his estate, without accusation or trial, would be so gross and notorious an act of despotism, as must at once convey the alarm of tyranny throughout the whole kingdom; but confinement of the person, by secretly hurrying him to jail, where his sufferings are unknown or forgotten, is a less public, a less striking, and therefore a more dangerous engine of arbitrary government. (1 Black. Com., 136.)

It may not be inappropriate, and, indeed, may be very necessary, before entering into the following discussion, to present a succinct and short statement of the causes which led, in England, to the passage of the Acts which will be hereafter referred to, so that the reader may have a better and clearer understanding of the same.

In retracing with care those foot-prints left in the sands of time by those who have preceded us in the weary pilgrimage of life, it cannot fail to strike the observant reader with peculiar force, that endeavors have been constantly made, as civilization advances, to place the good of the many above that of the few—the people, as a mass, above their governors; and to illustrate practically the remark of the historian, Livy, that "the common good is the great chain which binds men together in society." But, more especially is this true of those whose blood is running in the veins of most of us; for, although our remote ancestors were barbarians, acting, usually, under the command of some predatory chieftain, yet within their breasts they nurtured a love of liberty as vital as that to which we, as their descendants, have fallen heir. It is not then, astonishing, to one who has read with attention the early history of those whose blood is ours, to see them performing that great act in English history—and, we might justly say, in that of the world—at Runnymede, wresting from a weak but arbitrary King those liberties to which they were entitled, and of which their descendants should be proud. "The people," says Baron Verulam, referring to the early accounts of the Government of Britain, "held the helm of government in their own power;" and, remarks the learned Selden, alluding to the Saxons, "were a free people, governed by laws which they themselves made, and for this reason were denominated free."

1. MAGNA CHARTA, or the great Charter of the Liberties of Englishmen, and of us as their descendants, which, Sir Edward Coke says, "was, for the most part, declaratory of the principal grounds of the fundamental laws of England; and, for the residue, is additional, to supply some defects of the common law." (2 Inst., *proeme*, and pp. 65, 77, 78, 108,) was obtained from King John, A. D. 1215, at Running or Runnymede, a meadow, which derived its name either from a stream which flowed through it, or from the fact that many councils had been formerly held there. It is also bearing the name of Council Meadow, the Saxon word Rune signifying Council.

"There is no transaction in the ancient part of our English history," remarks Sir William Blackstone, "more interesting and important than the rise and progress, the gradual mutation and final establishment of the Charter of Liberties."

This instrument, although in the form of a grant from the Sovereign, was but an agreement on his part that, in future, those rights and liberties to which his subjects were by birthright entitled should be observed. The embryo of this Charter, or, as it might more correctly be called, Petition of Right, may be found in the Charters of Henry I. and Stephen. "It either granted or secured very important liberties and privileges to every order of men in the kingdom—to the clergy, to the barons, and to the people." (Hume, Hist. of Eng., vol. i., p. 194.) The first part related to the oppressions of the barons under the feudal law; the latter to the rights of the people, and "involves all the chief outlines of legal government, and provides for the equal distribution of justice and free enjoyment of property—the great objects for which political society was at first founded by men, which the people have a perpetual and unalienable right to recall, and which no time, nor precedent, nor statute, nor positive institution, ought to deter them from keeping ever uppermost in their thoughts and attention." (Ibid.)

"As the gold-finer," says Edward Coke, commenting on this Charter, "will not, out of the dust, threads, or shreds of gold, let pass the least crumb, in respect of the excellency of the metal, so ought not the learned reader to let pass any syllable of this LAW in respect of the matter."

The principal clause in this memorable instrument, chapter 39th, is in the following words:—

"NULLUS LIBER HOMO capiatur, vel imprisonetur, aut disseisiatur de libero tenemento suo, vel libertatibus, vel liberis consuetidinibus suis, aut utlagetur, aut exulet, aut aliquo modo destruatur; nec super eum ibimus, nec super eum mittemus, nisi per legale judicium parium suorum vel per legem terræ. Nulli vendemus, nulli negabimus, aut defferemus rectum, vel justiciam."

That is: "No freeman shall be taken or imprisoned, or be disseised of his freehold, or liberties, or free customs, or be outlawed or exiled, or any otherwise destroyed, nor we will pass upon him, nor condemn him, but by lawful judgment of his peers, or by the law of the land. We will sell to no man, we will not deny or defer to any man either justice or right."

"The King was, after this," to use the words of Holinshed, (Chron., vol. ii., p. 322,) "right sorrowfull in his heart, curssed his mother that bare him, the houre that he was borne, and the paps that gaue him sucke, wishing that he had receiued death by violence of sword or knife, in steed of naturall nourishment; he whetted his teeth; he did bite now on one staffe, and now on an other, as he walked, and oft brake the same in pieces when he had doone; and with such disordered behauiour and furious gestures he uttered his greefe, in such sorte that the noble men verie well perceiued the inclination of his inward affection concerning these things, before the breaking vp of the councell, and therefore sore lamented the state of the realme, gessing what would come of his impatiencie and displesant taking of the matter."

We cannot, in this connection, avoid quoting from the speech of the first Earl of Chatham, delivered in the House of Lords, January, 1770, in the case of John Wilkes, turned out of Parliament on account of his opinions. Commenting on the Great Charter, he said: "It is to your ancestors, my Lords, it is to the English Barons that we are indebted for the laws and Constitution we possess. I think that history has not done justice to their conduct, when they obtained from their sovereign that great acknowledgment of national rights contained in Magna Charta; they did not confine it to themselves alone, but delivered it as a common blessing to the whole people. They did not say, these are the rights of the great barons, or these are the rights of the great prelates. No, my Lords; they said, in the simple Latin of the times, *nullus liber homo*, (no free man,) and provided as carefully for the meanest subject as for the greatest. These are uncouth words, and sound but poorly in the ears of scholars; neither are they addressed to the criticism of scholars, but to the hearts of freemen. These three words, "*nullus liber homo*," have a meaning which interests us all. They deserve to be remembered; they deserve to be inculcated in our minds; *they are worth all the classics.*"

(See also, the eloquent remarks of Sir James Mackintosh, in his History of England.)

The effect of the chapter cited upon the subject hereafter discussed will appear from the following remarks by a celebrated writer on Constitutional law. We allude to Mr. Henry Hallam. "From the era of King John's Charter," he remarks, "it must have been a clear principle of our Constitution, that no man can be detained in prison without trial. Whether courts of justice framed the writ of Habeas Corpus in conformity to the spirit of this clause, or found it already in their register, it became, from that era, the right of every subject to demand it. That writ, rendered more actively remedial by the statute of Charles II., but founded upon the broad basis of Magna Charta, is the *principal bulwark of English liberty;* and if ever temporary circumstances, or the *doubtful plea of political necessity, shall lead men to look on its denial with apathy*, the most distinguishing characteristic of our Constitution will be effaced." (Hallam, Mid. Ages, vol. ii., p. 39.)

John died, A. D., 1216, and the Earl of Pembroke, Mareschall of England, by his office, was at the head of the army, as a consequence, during this period—one of convulsions and civil war—at the head of the Government. His first act was to renew the Great Charter, with some changes. It was renewed the next year by Henry, with some additions; and was also renewed at Oxford, A. D., in 1224, the ninth year of the King's reign. And, by the statute called *confirmatio cartarum*, [28 Edw. I., A. D., 1299,] the great Charter is directed to be observed as the Common Law of the realm. "All judgments contrary to it are declared void; copies of it are ordered to be sent to all cathedral churches, and read twice a year to the people; and sentence of excommunication is directed to be as constantly denounced against all those that in any degree infringe it." (Black. Com., vol. i., p. 128.)

To secure the observance of the Charters, the nobles and great officers were required to be sworn to observe them. (Coke, 2 Inst., *proeme.*) And every English monarch, at his coronation, is, at present, sworn to maintain them. (Wester. Comm., 142.) And, by the statute 25 Edw. I., all persons are to be excommunicated who, "by word, deed, or council, do contrary" thereto; are accursed, "and from the body of our Lord Jesus Christ," said the Archbishop, in the curse, "and from all the company of heaven, and from all the sacraments of Holy Church, are sequestered and excluded." This did not have the effect contemplated, for Coke reckons thirty-two confirmations from 9th Hen. III. (Hal. Mid. Ages, vol. ii., p. 40.) By statute 28 Edw. III., ch. 3, (A. D. 1354,) it is provided that "No man, of what state or condition that he be, shall be put out of land or tenement, nor taken, nor imprisoned, nor disinherited, nor put to death, without being brought in answer by the process of the law." And by statute made 5 Edw. III., ch. 9, (A. D. 1331,) "It is enacted that no man, from henceforth, shall be attached by any accusation, nor forejudged of life or limb, nor his lands, tenements, goods, &c., seised into the king's hands, against the form of the Great Charter *and the law of the land.*"

"All that has since been obtained," says Hallam, "is little more than a confirmation or commentary, (i. e., of Magna Charta;)

and if every subsequent law were to be swept away, there would still remain the bold features that distinguish a free from a despotic monarchy."

After a long interval, notorious for disputes between arbitrary Kings, Tudors and Stuarts, and a Parliament composed of men rapidly advancing in civilization, learning, and a knowledge of their rights—during which the Great Charter was frequently overlooked by the Sovereign, and illegal jurisdiction assumed by Judges holding office *durante beneplacito*—came the reign of that unfortunate Monarch, Charles the First—a man who did not understand the temper of the times, who acted upon bad advice, for the purpose, as he imagined, of retaining the prerogatives of the Crown—a period of the greatest interest to the student of Historical Jurisprudence.

2. THE PETITION OF RIGHT.

The action of the King in imprisoning certain of the gentry, and the refusal of the Court of King's Bench to bail them, formed one of the grievances which produced the famous Petition of Right, (3 Car. 1,) which was presented to the King, May 29th, 1627, over four hundred years after the passage of the great Charter.

When his assent was obtained, the greatest joy was manifested. "Bonfires were kindled all over London, and the whole nation was thrown into a transport of joy." This did not continue long; the King dissolved the Parliament, and a few days after seized Elliot, Holles, Selden, Long, Strode and others, who, to use his words, "by their disobedient and seditious carriage, we and our regal authority and commandment have been so highly contemned as our kingly office cannot bear, nor any former age can parallel."

Those in favor of the Parliament at that period, argued that "Privileges in particular, which are founded on the Great Charter, must always remain in force, because derived from the most sacred contract between the king and the people. Our generous ancestors,'" said they, "got the confirmation of it—the Great Charter—reiterated thirty several times. They have established it as a maxim, that even a statute, which should be enacted in contradiction to any article, cannot have force and validity." (Hume's England, chap. 51.)

The statute is called the Petition of Right, because not drawn in the common form of an Act of Parliament.

It enacts, among other things, that no freeman shall be imprisoned or detained without cause shown, to which he may make answer according to law.

Under this arbitrary King arrests were frequent, and were usually made under orders from the illegal courts, which he claimed to have the right to establish. By the Act—16 Car. 1, c. 10—abolishing the court of Star Chamber, every person committed contrary to that Act, or by the warrant of the King, the Council Board,

&c., upon demand unto the Court of King's Bench or Common Pleas in open court, was entitled, without delay, to a Writ of Habeas Corpus; and if any thing was willfully done or omitted to be done by any judge, &c., he was to forfeit to the party grieved treble damages. Under this Act, the Judges had a discretion as to bailing or discharging. This statute did away with the right of the King or Privy Council to arrest by warrant, but it seems they have that power at the present time. (Tomlin L. Dict. Title Commitment.)

3. THE WRIT OF HABEAS CORPUS.

The Writ is so called because of the Latin words of the Writ, commanding the party holding a person imprisoned legally or illegally, that he "have the body" of the prisoner before the power issuing it, at a certain day therein named, "*ad faciendum, subjiciendum et recipiendum*"—to do, submit to, and receive whatsoever the Judge or power awarding the Writ shall consider in that behalf. This Writ is somewhat similar to the Prætorian Interdict of the Roman Civil Law, "*De homino libero exhibendo*," in which the Prætor ordered, when it was made to appear to him that a freeman was restrained of his liberty, contrary to good faith, that he be liberated—this was called an "Exhibitory Interdict. (Sandars' Justinian, 590, Dig. 43, 29–1.) See, also, the Spanish process of "*de manifestacion*," a full description of which may be found in Hallam's Middle Ages, chap. iv.

It issues out of some of the English courts by the Common Law, but it was the statute of 31 Charles II., which brought it into frequent use. There was also issuing out of the courts, at the same time, other writs for the relief of an imprisoned person,—such were the writs of Mainprize, *De odio et atia and De Homine repleqiando* (3 Black. Com. 128,) all attesting the care with which the liberty of the subject was guarded from the earliest times. "The incapacity of these three remedies to give complete relief in every case," writes Justice Blackstone, 1765, "hath almost entirely antiquated them, and hath caused a general recourse to be had, in behalf of persons aggrieved by illegal imprisonment, to the Writ of Habeas Corpus." (Ibid. 129.)

The earliest case to be found in England is in the Year Books, Vine's case, 34 Hen. VI., although there is one which seems to refer to the Writ, 48 Edw. III., 22, where it is called *corpus cum causa*, (Hurd on H. C., p. 145.) It is issued in the name of the King in England, for he has a "right to be informed of the state and condition of every prisoner, and for what reason he is confined." (1 Chit. Cr. Law, 119, 5 Howard, 108, per Betts, J.) In this country, it is issued in the name of the Commonwealth. In England it is necessary, by statute, to have endorsed on the Writ that no one may plead ignorance—"*Per Statutem Tricesimo primo Caroli Secundi Regis.*"

4. THE HABEAS CORPUS ACT, 31 CHARLES II., c. 2.

Beside the arrests and detainers already mentioned, other abuses were daily practised—the Judges claimed a discretionary power as to granting the Writ or releasing under it; the jailer might delay a return till a *pluries*, or third writ, had been issued; and "many other vexatious shifts were practised to detain State prisoners in custody." (3 Blk. Com. 135.)

The Resolutions of Coke, 1628, and these abuses, produced the famous Habeas Corpus Act, 31 Car. II., c. 2, this Act having been made to prevent them. "I have already," writes Mr. Henry Hallam, (Cons. His., vol. 3, ch. 13,) "pointed out to the reader's notice that article of Clarendon's impeachment, which charges him with having caused many persons to be imprisoned against law. These were released by Buckingham's administration, which, in several respects, acted on a more liberal principle than any other in this reign. The practice was not wholly discontinued;" and after referring to the case of Jenkes, mentioned by Mr. Binney, p. 22, "This," he goes on to say, "has been commonly said to have produced the famous Act of Habeas Corpus. But this is not truly stated. The arbitrary proceedings of Lord Clarendon were what really gave rise to it. A bill to prevent the refusal of the writ was brought into the House on April 10th, 1668, but did not pass the committee in that session. But another to the same purpose, probably more remedial, was sent up to the Lords, March, 1669–70. It failed of success in the Upper House; but the Commons continued to repeat their struggle for this important measure, and, in the session of 1673-4, passed two bills—one to prevent the imprisonment of the subject in jails beyond the seas, another to give a more expeditious use of the writ of Habeas Corpus in criminal matters. The same or similar bills appear to have gone up to the Lords in 1675. It was not till 1676, that the delay of Jenkes' Habeas Corpus took place. And this affair seems to have had so stifling an influence that these bills were not revived for the next two years, notwithstanding the tempests that agitated the House during that period. But in the short Parliament of 1679, they appear to have been consolidated into one, that having met with better success among the Lords, passed into a statute, and is generally denominated the Habeas Corpus Act."

The case of Jenkes, July 28, 1676, arose upon a refusal of the Chancellor Nottingham, because of alleged want of power, to issue the Writ in vacation, this and the difficulties and delays thrown in the way of his release by the Chief Justice of the King's Bench attracted considerable attention at the time. The decision of the Chancellor has been since overruled (1818) by Lord Eldon, in Crowley's case. (2 Swanston, 1.) Perhaps Jenkes case, and the fear that the Duke of York was not of the Established Church, helped to produce the Act; yet it should be borne in mind that Parliaments were held, 1677, January 28th, adjourned

March 21st; May 21st, adjourned 28th. 1678: April 24th, prorogued May 13th; May 22d, prorogued July 15; October 21st, prorogued December 30th; March 6th, prorogued May 27th. 1679: it was this one passed 31 Charles, which received the Royal assent, May 9th, 1679.

"Whoever will attentively consider the English history, may observe, that the flagrant abuse of any power, by the Crown or its ministers, has always been productive of a struggle; which either discovers the exercise of that power to be contrary to law, or, if legal, restrains it for the future," (3 Black. Com. 135,) or, to use the more expressive language of Coke, in his speech on the Petition of Right, "Magna Charta is such a fellow, that he will have no sovereign."

The author of this Act was Anthony Ashley Cooper, first Earl of Shaftesbury. A curious circumstance, as to its passage, is related by Burnet, (*vide* His. of his Times, vol. 1, ch. 2.)

It enacts, section 2d, That every sheriff, &c., within three days after the service of the Writ of Habeas Corpus, is to obey it, unless the commitment is for treason or felony, plainly and specially expressed in the warrant of commitment; and by section 21, as accessory, or on suspicion of being accessory, before the fact, to any petit treason or felony, plainly expressed in the warrant; or unless convicted or charged in execution by legal process.

By Sec. 3d every Writ is to be marked—that it issues by this statute, and is it enacted that any person detained as aforesaid, for any crime, except the above specified in the vacation time or out of term, or any one in his or their behalf, may complain in writing, to the Chancellor or any of the Judges, &c.; and he or any of them, upon view of the copy or copies of the warrant or warrants, or upon oath made, that such copies were denied to be given by those detaining, are to award and grant an Habeas Corpus, under the seal of the court, directed to the officer, &c., detaining, returnable immediately; and on service, the officer, &c., shall bring such prisoner within the times before limited before such Chancellor, or one or all of said Judges, with the return of the Writ, and the true causes of commitment and detainer; and thereupon, within two days after the party shall be brought before them, he or they shall discharge the prisoner from his imprisonment, taking surety, unless it appears that the person is detained upon legal process, order or warrant, issued out of some court having jurisdiction.

By Sec. 6th no person, once delivered by Habeas Corpus, shall be recommitted for the same offence, by other than a court having jurisdiction of the cause, under penalty of £500; but this will not prevent recommitment for same offence on new evidence.

By Sec. 7th, if any one committed for treason or felony, expressed in the warrant, upon his petition in court the first week of the term, or first day of the sessions of Oyer and Terminer, to be brought to trial, shall not be indicted, some time in the next term, it shall and may be lawful for the Judges of the King's Bench, &c., and they are required to discharge the prisoner upon motion the last day of the term, unless it appear to them that the witnesses for the King could not be produced; and if not tried the second term, he is to be discharged from his imprisonment.

By Sec. 10th, if the Writ is *denied* by any of the Judges, &c., they shall forfeit £500.

And lest this Act might be evaded, by demanding excessive bail, it was enacted by Statute 1 W. & M. St. 2, c. 2, (A. D. 1689,) that excessive bail ought not to be required.

This Act gave no new rights or privileges to the people; it only rendered secure the provisions of the Great Charter; for those provisions were a nullity without the Writ of Habeas Corpus, or some process of the law having the same effect. It has been enacted, in words or in substance, according to Chancellor Kent, in every State of the Union, and is "the basis of all the American statutes on the subject."

"We must admire, as the keystone of civil liberty, the statute which forces the secrets of every prison to be revealed, the cause of every commitment to be declared, and the person of the accused to be produced, that he may claim his enlargement, or his trial within a limited time. No wiser form was ever opposed to the abuses of power. But it requires a fabric no less than the whole political constitution of Great Britain, *a spirit no less than the refractory and turbulent zeal of this fortunate people, to secure its effects.*" (Ferguson on Civil Society, p. 302.) The object of this statute was to secure the benefit of the writ—the right to it—the privilege of it—rather than extend its operation. (North Am. Rev., Oct., 1861, p. 479.)

5. THE BILL OF RIGHTS

Was passed, 1689, on the accession of William III. It had been preceded by a Declaration of Rights, February 18th of that year, which declared, among other things:—that the power of suspending laws without the consent of Parliament, is illegal; that the pretended power of dispensing with laws by Royal authority, as it hath been assumed and exercised of late, is illegal; that excessive bail ought not to be required, nor excessive fines imposed, nor cruel and unusual punishments inflicted; that the raising or keeping of a standing army within the kingdom, in time of peace, unless it be with consent of Parliament, is illegal; that the subjects which are Protestants may have arms for their defence, suitable to their condition, and as allowed by law; and a number of other provisions, we have not space to mention.

"The Declaration of Right," remarks Macaulay, (Hist. of Eng., vol. 2, p. 518,) "though it made nothing law which had not been law before, contained the germ of the law which gave religious freedom to the Dissenter, of the law which secured the independence of the Judges, of the law which limited the duration of Parliaments, of the law which placed the liberty of the press under the protection of juries, of the law which prohibited the slave trade, of the law which abolished the sacramental test, of the law which relieved Roman Catholics from civil disabilities, of the law which reformed the representative system, of every good law which had been passed during one hundred and sixty years, of every good law which hereafter, in the course of ages, may be found necessary to promote the public weal, and to satisfy the demands of public opinion."

This Declaration was confirmed some months after by Parliament as the Bill of Rights: the latter contained one clause, however, extending beyond it. The Lords had added to the clause relating to the dispensing power, the words "As it has been exercised of late." In the bill a clause was inserted "that no dispensation by *non obstante* to any statute should be allowed, except in such cases as should be especially provided for by a bill to be passed during the present session." This reservation went to satisfy the scruples of the Lords. (Hallam, Cons. Hist., vol. 3, c. 15.) This bill was never passed. (Ibid.)

6. STATUTE 56 GEO. III., c. 100.

"In the year 1757 the Act of Charles II. came under discussion in both Houses of Parliament, upon the following occasion:—A gentleman having been impressed before the Commissioners under a pressing-act passed in the preceding session, and confined in the Savoy, his friends made application for a Writ of Habeas Corpus, which produced some hesitation and difficulty; for, according to the above statute, the *privilege* relates only to persons committed for criminal, or supposed criminal matters, and this gentleman did not stand in that predicament. Before the question could be determined, he was discharged, in consequence of an application to the Secretary of War; but, the nature of the case seeming to point out a defect in the Act, a bill for giving a more speedy remedy to the subject upon the Writ was prepared and presented to the Commons." (English Ed. note to Bac. Abrg't. Hab. Corp.) The bill was passed by the Commons, but was thrown out in the House of Lords at the second reading. The debates in the latter are remarkable for the ground against the liberty of the subject, taken by Lord Mansfield. (Campbell's Lives of the C. Justices, vol. ii., p. 346, A. D. 1757, and Debrett's Deb., vol. vii., App'x.)

Mansfield, whilst in the Lords, was always the champion of the King's prerogative, and upon this occasion made the following remarks: "That people supported it (i. e., the Writ of Habeas Corpus,) from the groundless imagination that liberty was concerned in it, whereas it had as little to do with liberty as the navigation laws or the act for the encouragement of madder; that ignorance on subjects of this nature was extremely pardonable, since the knowledge of laws required a particular study of them; that the greatest genius, without such study, could no more become master of them than of Japanese literature, without understanding the language of the country; and that sufficient remedy against all those abuses this bill was supposed to rectify."

This speech convinced many persons. "Nor did I know how true a votary I was to liberty," writes Horace Walpole, "till I found I was not one of the number staggered by that speech." (Mem. of Geo. II., vol. ii., p. 30.)

Mansfield was the Judge who decided the case of the slave Sommersett, (1 How. St. Tr., 2,) on the ground that slaves could not breathe in England. (*vide* Arg't of Mr. Hargrave in that case, and 2 Hagg. Ad. Rep., 105.)

The Judges were ordered to prepare a bill to extend the power of granting the Writ, in vacation, in cases not within the statute of Charles. The matter was, however, neglected.

By 56 Geo. III., c. 100, (A. D. 1816,) it is enacted that if any person is confined or restrained of his liberty, (except for crime or debt,) any Judge shall, on complaint on behalf of such person, if reasonable cause appear to him, award, in vacation time, a writ of Habeas Corpus *ad subjiciendum*, returnable immediately. The Judge may then examine the truth of the fact in the return, and do therein as to justice shall appertain; or, if he has any doubt, may bail the person detained to appear before the court. The party refusing to obey the Writ is declared guilty of a contempt of court, and may be arrested and held for such contempt. The provisions of the Act are also extended to Writs awarded in pursuance of former existing Acts. This statute was, no doubt, the result of the attempt made in 1757. (See further, Hal. Cons. His., vol. ii., p. 11.)

7. SUSPENSION IN ENGLAND.

It is sometimes considered necessary, in England, to suspend the effect of this Writ for a limited time; and it is strange what a confusion of ideas has resulted from the power. The Constitution of Great Britain exists in the breast of Parliament; it is unwritten. It is therefore considered to be within the power of Parliament to suspend the operation of the Act of 31 Charles II. Blackstone says: "It is the Parliament only, or legislative power, can authorize the crown, by suspending the Habeas Corpus Act for a short and limited time, to imprison suspected persons without giving any reason for so doing." (1 Blk. Com., 136.) Others say, in the Debates, (*vide* Cobbett's and Hansard's Parl. Deb.,) suspend the Writ; suspend the privilege of the Writ; the Habeas Corpus, without anything added; one, the peculiarity of the Constitution of this country is, that "the privilege of the Writ of Habeas

Corpus" is to be suspended. In Great Britain the Writ is really never suspended. The words of the statute there are, that the persons imprisoned "may be detained in safe custody, without bail or mainprize, until," &c.; not that the Writ shall not issue. Arrests are perfectly legal, in England, if made by the warrant of the Privy Council or Secretaries of State, if the case be an extraordinary one. (4 Blk. Com., 290; Tom. L. D., vol. i., 363, 364.) The effect of the Writ does not appear to have been suspended until 1689. (Macaulay's Hist. of Eng., vol. iii., pp. 38, 316.) It was then suspended by statutes, 1 W. & M., sess. 1, c. 2 and c. 7. (These were bills to detain only. Stat. at Large, vol. iii., p. 417.) By c. 19; (Ibid, 427) and c. 21; (Ibid, 603.) The Privy Council and Ministers having, on various occasions—there being, at the time, no suspension of the Writ—arrested suspected persons, (*vide* Macaulay, vol. iii., p. 478, among other instances,) the Parliament, in 1690, passed an Act 2 W. & M., c. 13; (9 Stat. at Large, 212) indemnifying the Ministers therefor. (Burnett's Hist. of his own Times, pp. 562, 585.) The Ministers acted subject to punishment by the Parliament, Parliament afterwards indemnified them.

"A great mistake exists as to the extent of this bill," said Lord Thurlow, in debating a bill suspending the effect of the Writ, "which, in fact, gives no power to the executive government, as to confining and detaining suspected persons, which they had not before, except this, that they could not be so secured and detained for a certain time without being brought to trial. Why it had vulgarly been called a suspension of the Habeas Corpus Act he could not tell; and yet it had been so called almost every time that a bill of this sort had been brought forward; for, if this bill was passed to-morrow, the Habeas Corpus Act still would remain in force; and magistrates must consider that to be the case," and act at their peril. (Cobbett's Deb., vol. xxxi., p. 587.)

"In the reign of Queen Anne" (the effect) "was suspended twice; and during the reign of the first two branches of the House of Brunswick it was suspended more than once. I find that, from the Revolution down to the treaty of Aix-la-Chapelle, this important *privilege* was not withdrawn from the British people so often as it has been during the very few years of this (Mr. Pitt's) administration." (C. J. Fox, Cob. Deb., vol. iii., p. 327.)

Another member of the House remarked, upon another occasion, that, within one hundred and twenty-four years, the Writ had been suspended nine or twelve times. (Cob. Deb., vol. xxxvii., p. 462.)

The American people took the idea of suspending this valuable privilege, doubtless, from these Acts and the Statute 17 Geo. III., c. 9, 1777, (Stat. at Large, vol. xiii., p. 18,) which applied to them especially. By it, persons who had been, or might thereafter be, arrested in America for high treason, or on the high seas for piracy, or who were charged with, or suspected of, the crime of high treason, or, on the high seas, of piracy; and who have been or shall be committed, in any part of his Majesty's dominions, for such crimes, or for suspicion, by any magistrate having competent authority, to the common jail, &c., "shall and may be thereupon secured and detained in safe custody, without bail or mainprize," till January 1, 1778. By the 4th section, the Act was not to apply to any person committing the said crimes within the realm.

The usual method of suspending the effect of the Writ in England is to be found in the Statute 57 Geo. III., ch. 3. (St. at Large, vol. 25, p. 2,) March 4, 1817, entituled, "An Act to empower his Majesty to secure and detain such persons as his Majesty shall suspect of conspiring against his Person and Government." It recites that "a traitorous conspiracy had been formed for the purpose of overthrowing, by means of a general insurrection, the established Government, laws, and constitution of the kingdom;" and that designs and practices, of a treasonable and highly dangerous nature, were then being carried on in London and other parts of Great Britain, for the better preservation of his Majesty's person, and that of the Prince Regent, and for securing the peace and laws and liberties of the kingdom, it was enacted by the King, Lords and Commons. "That all or any person or persons that are or shall be in prison in Great Britain, at or upon the day on which this Act receive his Majesty's Royal assent, or after, by warrant of his said Majesty's most honorable Privy Council, signed by six of said Privy Council, for high treason, suspicion of high treason, or treasonable practices, by warrant signed by his Majesty's Secretaries of State, for such causes as aforesaid, may be detained in safe custody, without bail or mainprize, until, &c.; and no Judge or Justice of the Peace shall bail or try any such person or persons committed, without order from said Privy Council, until, &c., any law or statute to the contrary notwithstanding."

By Sec. III. That from and after . . . the said persons so committed shall have the benefit and advantage of all laws, &c., relating to or providing for the liberty of the subjects of the realm.

By Sec. IV. That nothing therein was to "be construed to extend to or invalidate the ancient rights and privileges of Parliament, or to the imprisonment or detaining of any member of either House during the sitting of Parliament, "until the charge be communicated to the House, and their consent to such detaining be obtained." This Act was repealed before its limitation expired.

A statute was also passed, in a different form, in Ireland, (1798,) in which the privilege of the Writ is granted. (Sim. on Courts Martial, 631, q. v.)

The situation of the people of England, under this statute, "was, that any person committed by a warrant, signed by any of his Majesty's Secretaries of State, or by six Privy Counsellors, for high treason, or treasonable practices, could not be bailed or brought to trial without the consent of six Privy Counsellors." (Sir Samuel Romilly, Cob. Deb., vol. 35, p. 785.)

The abuses under these suspensions were very great; for instance, in 1818, the petitions of some twenty-one persons, illegally imprisoned, claiming that their cases might be heard, and that they were innocent, were presented to Parliament. (Cob. Deb., vol. 37.) And in 1817, Sir Francis Burdett said, "He well recollected what had been done by former ministers who had been invested with the undue power, proposed to be bestowed on the noble lord and his colleagues. Under their authority, innocent men had been confined for years in dismal and unhealthy dungeons. A young man," said he, "had been detained seven years; and the noble Viscount Sidmouth, who would have an inforcement of this bill, procured a law to be passed to prevent all persons from suing for indemnification." (Cob. Deb. 35, p. 750.) And a member mentioned, on another occasion, a case in which a man had been detained, upon a warrant from the King, for over forty years.

HISTORY OF THE WRIT IN AMERICA.

Having thus considered the origin and history of the Writ in England, whence we derive it, we now come to the second branch of the subject, THE HABEAS CORPUS IN AMERICA, and herein—

1st. MAGNA CHARTA IN AMERICA.

The Governments of the American colonies were Charter, Royal or Provincial, and Proprietary. The charter Governments existed only in New England; they conferred the right of the soil, and the privileges of natural born subjects—the laws were not to be contrary to those of England. The Royal or Provincial Governments were those of Virginia, New York, New Hampshire, New Jersey, the Carolinas, (then one province) and Georgia; these Governments were called Royal, because they derived their powers directly from the Crown, the Governors held their offices at its pleasure, and acted under its instructions—and all laws were subject to the negative of the Governor, and all acts, though approved by him before they could become laws, must have been first approved of by the King. The Proprietary Governments were those of Maryland, Pennsylvania, Delaware, and at first the Carolinas and Jerseys—the authority of the proprietors within their own Governments was nearly equal to that of the Crown in the Royal Governments—they appointed the Governors, and had the right to repeal all laws made by the Assemblies; the proprietors were, however, subject to the control of the Crown, from whom their powers were derived.

"In their most solemn declaration of rights," says Justice Story, "they admitted themselves bound, as British subjects, to allegiance to the British Crown; and as such, they claimed to be entitled to all the rights, liberties and immunities of free-born British subjects."

In the grants from the Crown, it was expressly mentioned, with the exception of Pennsylvania, in which grant equivalent words are used, that all subjects and their children, inhabiting the colonies, were to be deemed natural born subjects, and as such, entitled to the rights and liberties thereof. In the Congress held 1765, in New York, it was asserted that the colonists were "entitled to all the inherent rights and liberties of his (the King's) natural born subjects, within the kingdom of Great Britain." In the Continental Congress, 1774, it is declared, "That the inhabitants of the English colonies of North America, by the immutable laws of nature, the principles of the English Constitution, and the several charters and compacts, have the following rights:—

That our ancestors, who first settled these colonies, were, at the time of their emigration from the mother country, entitled to all the rights, liberties and immunities of free and natural born subjects within the realm of England." (Amer. Arch., 911.)

The colonies "are equally entitled with yourselves," said Chatham, (Speech on Taxing America,) "to all the natural rights of mankind, and the peculiar *privileges of Englishmen;* equally bound by the laws, and equally participating in the constitution of this free country. The Americans are the sons, not the bastards, of England." There can be no doubt in the mind of the reader of colonial history, that Magna Charta, especially Chapter 39th, was in force.

2d. THE WRIT OF HABEAS CORPUS IN AMERICA.

The first account we have found of an attempt to use the Writ in America, was in a case which occurred in Massachusetts, 1689, in which the application was refused. (Washburn's Judicial Hist. of Mass., 196.)

By Act of 1692, under the Province Charter, the Judges of the Supreme Court had power given them to grant Writs of Habeas Corpus. (Ibid. 152.) This appears to have been disallowed in 1695. The first instance of an application for the Writ, after this, was in 1706. (Ibid. 196.)

It appears, by the same book, that the Judge was sued for refusing it, "which shows that the right to this Writ was regarded as one of the existing privileges of the colonies."

The Rev. John Wise, who had applied, was arrested with others for refusing to grant money, which they deemed the Governor and the Council to have assessed illegally. "Being denied the Writ, the mittimus only showing that they were committed for contempts and high misdemeanors, they were, after a tedious delay, put upon trial. They claimed the *privileges* secured to them as Englishmen by the Magna Charta and the laws of England. The Chief Justice, however, informed them that they must not expect that the laws of England would follow them to the ends of the earth, and concluded by telling them they had no more privileges left than to be sold as slaves. He charged the jury, and stated that the court expected a good verdict, seeing the matter had been sufficiently proven against criminals. A verdict was accordingly rendered against them, and a severe punishment inflicted, because the town in which they resided declined yielding to an arbitrary and illegal act." (Ibid., 116—see, also, 4 Force's Hist. Tract. Acct. of Rev. in N. Eng., 1689.) In South Carolina the Act of Charles II. appears to have been adopted, 1692. (Hewitt's Hist. of South Car., 116.) As to Virginia (see Chalmers' An., vol. 1.) In Maryland there was no Act; but the Statute of Charles appears to have been adopted, in conformity to the practice of adopting statutes applicable to the state of the colonies. (*Vide* Report to Legislature, 1810, and 1 Kent Com. 473.) In New Jersey, 1710, the Assembly animadverted severely on the course of one of the Judges for having refused the Writ to one Thomas Gordon, saying it was the "undoubted right and great privilege of the subject." (Colonial Courts of New Jersey, 76.) In New York the first Writ appears to have been issued, March, 1707; and under it prisoners were bailed. (Vide Pamphlet in 4 Force's Hist. Tracts—Trial of Makemie.)

The Statute of Charles does not appear to be in force in the State of Pennsylvania. (Rob. Dig., p. 75, note.) That State was not settled, however, till 1682. The Statute of Charles was passed in 1679. (See, however, Galloway's Laws, 1; Col. Rec., 374; 1 Smith's Laws, 56; 2 Ibid., 275; and Statutes as to Bailing, Rob. Dig.) An early case, likely on the subject, is to be found 1 Col. Rec., 24. It may therefore be advanced as undoubted, that at the time the Constitution of 1787 went into effect, the right or privilege of the Writ was a privilege attached to an existing legal Writ in all the States.

The Writ issues out of the United States courts, by virtue of the Acts of Congress, September 24th, 1789, Sec. 14; (2 Story's L. of U. S., 62,) March 2, 1833, Sec. 7; (4 Stat. at Large, 634,) August 29, 1842. (5 Ibid., 539.)

SUSPENSION OF THE PRIVILEGE OF THE WRIT IN AMERICA.

It does not appear, by the Declaration of our Independence, that the suspension of the privilege of the Writ was any cause for its adoption; indeed, the suspension, as to America, did not take place till 1777; but there are causes assigned in that instrument which were equivalent to its suspension. "He," (the King,) are its words, "has kept among us, in times of peace, standing armies, without the consent of our Legislatures. He has affected to render the military independent of, and superior to, the civil power. He has combined with others to subject us to a jurisdiction foreign to our Constitutions and unacknowledged by our laws, giving his assent to their acts of pretended legislation, for quartering large bodies of armed troops among us; for depriving us, in many cases, of the benefits of trial by jury; for transporting us beyond seas, to be tried for pretended offences, and abolishing our most valuable laws."

A reference is, however, made to the case of Canada. "For abolishing," it says, "the free system of English laws in a neighboring province, establishing therein an arbitrary government." This was the effect of what was called the "Quebec Bill," which did away with the right to the Writ of Habeas Corpus. (6 Bancroft, p. 527; 1 Am. Arch., 4th series, p. 170.) This bill was made ground of complaint by the Congress of 1774. (Ibid., pp. 920, 931.)

The first time the effect of the Writ was suspended in this country, after the acknowledgment of Independence, was in Massachusetts, November, 1786, in the rebellion in that State known as Shay's. It was then suspended for eight months. (Barry's Hist. of Mass., vol. iii., p. 235; Brad. Hist. of Mass., p. 316; Holl. Hist. of Mass., pp. 249–50.) The suspension was by the Legislature, not by the Governor, acting on his own authority. The following account is given by Minot, in his History of the Insurrection:

A meeting of the Legislature was called by the Governor. The first measure adopted by the Senate was to agree upon a report of a joint committee on the Governor's speech. This report provided that the privilege of the Writ of Habeas Corpus should be suspended for a limited time. (Minot, p. 51.) This clause was not agreed to by the House. The people who were opposed to the insurrection were alarmed at this, and the non-adoption of coercive measures. About the 7th of November a law was passed which empowered the Governor and Council to imprison, without bail or mainprize, any persons they should deem the safety of the Commonwealth required to be restrained of their liberty, or whose enlargement was dangerous thereto, the duration of which was limited to the 1st of July, 1787. This was following the British practice, suspending the effect of the Writ, not the privilege. The Constitution of the State (1780) has the words, suspension "of the privilege of the Writ."

Nothing was said on the subject in any of the Articles of Confederation; each State was left to manage its power over the Writ as it listed; but when those Articles were up for revision, in 1787, the attempt was first made to introduce such clause among the powers of the General Government.

By the third section of the "Act for the government and regulation of seamen in the merchant service," July 20, 1790, (2 Story's L. of U. S., p. 116,) if a vessel is returned to port on account of leakiness and refusal of the crew to proceed to sea in her, and it is ascertained that the complaint has no foundation—or the ship is prepared to go to sea, and the seamen refuse to go in her—"it shall and may be lawful for any justice of the peace to commit the seamen by warrant to the common gaol, to remain, without bail and mainprize, until," &c. "Nor shall any such seaman be discharged upon any Writ of habeas corpus, or otherwise, until, &c., for want of any form of commitment, or other previous proceedings. Provided, that sufficient matter shall be made to appear, upon the return of such habeas corpus and an examination then to be had, to detain him for the causes hereinbefore assigned." This shows that Congress has exercised the power of suspending the effect of the Writ.

An attempt was made to suspend the privilege during the time of the supposed treason of Aaron Burr. (1 Burr's Trial, p. 78.) The bill passed the Senate, January 23, 1807, but was rejected by the House. There is not any case, either in this country, or in England, in which it has been pretended, since 1689, except within the last few months, that any one had the right, but the Legislative power, to suspend the Writ, the effect of the Writ, or the privilege of the Writ. Not a word is said which implies that the President had any such power, in the debates of the ninth Congress, second session, though fifty-eight pages are devoted to the subject. Every writer is opposed to it; every feeling of the soul shrinks, and Liberty seems paralyzed, and stands aghast at the assertion.

THE PRIVILEGE OF THE WRIT UNDER THE CONSTITUTION.

A Constitution of Government, is a fundamental regulation or law, that determines the manner in which the public authority is to be executed. (Vattel, Bk. 1, ch. 3, s. 27; 4 Cranch. 93.) It may be written or unwritten. That of England is unwritten. The Constitution of the United States declares that it, and the laws made pursuant to it, are to "be the SUPREME LAW of the land." (Sec. 2, Art. VI.)

The Constitution of the United States, and those of the various States composing it, are written, but are different in effect and the powers under them. In construing the Constitution of the United States, to ascertain what powers are given, we examine to see what powers are expressly granted, or are necessarily implied for their exercise. In the State Constitutions, we only examine to see what are denied by the Federal and State Constitutions; the law-making power, without and beyond these, is as absolute, omnipotent, and uncontrollable as Parliament itself. (Mason vs. Waite, 4 Scammon, Ill. Rep. 134—see 11 Peters, 257; Sedg. on Const. and St. Law,

587.) "The Federal Constitution intends, however, to preserve the same lines of demarkation between the Executive, Legislative and Judicial powers, as those which the States have described." (Ibid., 590.)

Clause 2d, Section 9th, Article I. of the Constitution of the United States is in these words—viz.: "The privilege of the Writ of Habeas Corpus shall not be suspended, unless, when in cases of rebellion or invasion, the public safety may require it."

This clause is elliptical, and when the proper words are supplied, will read: "The privilege of the Writ of Habeas Corpus shall not be" *at any time* "suspended," *by the power having the right to suspend it,* "unless, when in cases of rebellion or invasion," *that power having then the right to suspend, shall deem* "the public safety may require it" *to be suspended, and then it may be suspended.*

The clause implies, 1st, That power is to exist to suspend the privilege of the Writ. 2d. That that power is to be curtailed, so that it shall not suspend the privilege, except the public safety requires it, in cases of rebellion and invasion; and that there existed, if nothing had been said in the Constitution about it—

1. A power existing which might suspend previous to the introduction of the clause.

2. A power to suspend subsequent to the introduction of the clause.

3. The fact that a suspension could take place, if no clause had been inserted.

4. The fact that a suspension could take place subsequent to the introduction of the clause, subject in second and fourth propositions, to the following contingencies:—

1. A rebellion, or
2. An invasion, and in both cases,
3. The public safety requiring it.

It also assumed the existence of the legal privilege of the Writ in the United States, and acted—

1. As a prohibition, on the suspension by the States of that legal privilege, the States, before it was passed, being only bound as to suspensions by their Constitutions, in some of which there was no provision for suspension and no guaranty of its inviolability.

2. As a prohibition on the Government of the United States, acting immediately when the clause went into effect, over the powers of the Government, relating to the privilege in the States, so that Congress could not suspend it until the happening of the required conditions, and in the future as to the privilege which was to be provided for by Congress. It also guarantied the privilege of the Writ, 1st, To citizens, so that under the United States and State Constitutions no suspension should take place except the condition should first happen upon which suspension could take place;

suspension then occurring, it abrogated the State Constitutions and laws, and the Constitution and laws of the United States, wherever they conflict with such suspension. It is also a question whether the clause did not give, to some extent, as well as guaranty, the Writ to the citizen; for if it did not, what would be his position if Congress had never given the power to the courts of the United States to issue such Writs? Could not arrests have been made by process of these courts, without the right of the prisoner to the privilege of the Writ, there being no existing Writ in such courts,—therefore a virtual suspension of it, in all cases of arrest under such process, contrary to the clause cited.

From the clause may also be deduced the following propositions:

1. The expression means the Privilege of Bail, Trial or Discharge, as though it had used those words.

2. That it is a personal privilege, applying to each person arrested, and not the community.

3. That it means Privilege generally of the Writ of Habeas Corpus, as a Writ known to the officers of the law, and applying to the community.

4. That it means a privilege of citizens of this country, as distinct from the rights of subjects of a foreign nation, under their own Governments, or as aliens under ours.

Mr. Binney uses the former two; attention will be therefore confined to the fact of the intent to use them, or the latter. It may be useful to a clear understanding of the subject, before proceeding further, to give some rules as to the interpretation of Statutes. The Rules of the Barons of the Exchequer (Haydon's case, 3 Rep. 7) were to look at and consider—

1. What was the Common Law before the making of the Act?

2. What was the mischief and defect against which the Common Law did not provide?

3. What remedy the Parliament hath resolved and appointed to cure the disease of the Commonwealth?

4. The true reason of the remedy.

And of the 1st. It "is the very lock and key to set open the windows of the Statute." By the Common Law, the Writ existed, and by it or statute was a legal writ in the States. Congress had the right under the power to establish courts, (Art. III.,) to give power to the Federal courts to issue Writs of Habeas Corpus, and would certainly have a right to suspend that power whenever they deemed it necessary.

2. The mischief against which there was no provision, was the right to suspend the Writ, *ad libitum*, by the State Governments, and by Congress, of the power to issue by the Federal courts.

3. The remedy is, that the privilege of the Writ is not to be suspended by any power anywhere, except in specified cases.

4. The reason of the remedy was that the Constitution, and the laws made in pursuance of it, were to be the Supreme Law of the

land, and they governed both the people, the State Governments, and that of the United States. Suspension might be necessary, owing to rebellion or an invasion. This power, vested in the United States, would make it cover the different States, if Congress deemed it essential, and would prevent the clashing of State interests and laws.

The argument of Mr. Binney is founded principally on the following propositions:

1. That the English Constitution, being unwritten, and the power of the King greater than that of our Executive, the power of Parliament supreme, and the word privilege used in our Constitution, English analogy as to the suspension is to be excluded from the argument, and such was the intent of the framers of the Constitution.

2. That the word "privilege," in the Constitution, is a term of description, meaning only a personal privilege attached to each person of bail, trial or discharge; therefore the Executive suspends as to each person individually.

3. That the acts of the Convention which framed the Constitution, of those which ratified it, and cotemporary exposition show that the intent was to discard the customary language of the day in this clause, and give the power to suspend to the Executive, not the Legislative branch of the Government; and that the argument from position is false.

4. That the Constitution authorizes suspension, and does not require a law to define or give it vitality.

5. That the power to suspend should be the one charged with the care of the public safety.

6. That impeachment is a sufficient check to prevent abuse of the power, if it be in the Executive, he having but few powers, and being the most amenable to punishment for abuse.

7. The right to arrest is also deduced from the right to suspend.

By the Constitution of Great Britain, Parliament is supreme; it can abrogate laws, and do away with liberties. A statute is there the highest authority. "It can do no wrong," says Lord Holt; "it may do several things that look pretty odd;" and says Vaughan, C. J., "it can make Malta in Europe, and can make a woman a Mayor or a Justice of the Peace." (2 Jones, Rep. 12.) The power of English Parliament is, therefore, different from that of Congress; but this is no proof that the people of this country meant to exclude Parliamentary analogy, in that part of their Constitution in which nothing is said. They have said the privilege shall not be suspended, except on certain conditions, and by this have restricted the power of that body which is founded on English analogy; that it was meant by this to exclude English precedents, when the case arises upon which no restrictions are placed, the whole spirit of our institutions shows it to be incorrect. It was intended to qualify those principles so that they should not apply as precedents in those qualified cases. In this clause the privilege of the Writ is not to be suspended, unless the fact of rebellion or invasion and the public safety should require it; this does not exclude, when those facts arise, the customs and law of England. The clause does not say, that no suspension shall take place, but that it may take place.

The difference between the English and our Constitution—that one is written, the other not—we shall not discuss very fully. The fact that one is written, the other unwritten, is of no importance, provided the effect be similar; and we can prove from our Constitution the intent to put the power of suspension in Legislative hands. English analogy is, however, cited by Mr. Binney to support his side of the question.

The proposition to which the attention of the reader will be confined, is the third given by Mr. Binney, in his introduction,—whether or not the power to suspend the Writ be "a civil power, springing from the Habeas Corpus clause of the Constitution, and to be authorized by Congress, in like manner as by the Parliament of England, by delegating to the President the power to *arrest* and *detain* persons, within the limitations prescribed by the Constitution." It is to this he principally directs his attention, and it will therefore be unnecessary to take any other text. He informs us that it is his intention "to consider the right of the President to *arrest and detain, of his own motion*, in the *required conditions*, as derived from the language of the Constitution, and from the nature of the Executive office." The sentence contains an ellipsis which, when supplied, makes the last sentence read—"from the nature of the Executive office," *derived from the language of the Constitution.* The Constitution is the governing power in both propositions; for all power is derived from it. This does not mean, however, that we are to look nowhere else for analogies, or that the strict letter is to be the governing principle. "He who sticks to the letter, sticks in the bark."

It will be, therefore, necessary to consider, 1st, The right of the President to arrest and detain, of his own motion, in the required conditions, as derived from the language of the Constitution. 2d. Under the same circumstances, but as derived from the nature of the Executive office. Under both of these propositions to consider,

1. The right of the President to arrest.
2. The right of the President to detain, and in both of these cases.
3. The right to arrest and detain of his own motion.

And 1st. THE RIGHT OF THE PRESIDENT TO ARREST, *as derived from the Constitution, subject to the conditions therein specified.* It is provided, in the amendments to the Constitution, that "No warrant shall issue, but upon probable cause, supported by oath or affirmation, and particularly describing the place to be searched, and the person or things to be seized." (Art. IV.) Under this clause, in Burford's case, (3 Cranch. Rep. 448,) the Supreme Court, U. S., held that a warrant of commitment was illegal, for not "stating some good cause certain supported by oath." This section was intended to guard against what are known in England as general warrants, of which there seem to be two kinds—one without the name of the party, and one without the charge specified. The right to the latter seems to be exploded; (Leache's Hawkins, P. C., 2, c. 13, § 10, and note;) and Blackstone holds to the opinion that the right to the former is also. But, notwithstanding the Constitution, an arrest may be made for felony without warrant, but it is at the risk of the person making it. (6 Binney, 316.) There is also another amendment (Art. V.) which enacts that "No person shall be deprived of life, liberty, or property, *without due process of law.*" This has been decided to mean judicial process. (3 Story on Cons., 661, *vide* Sharswood's Black. Com., vol. 1, p. 135, note.)

By the law of England, the King cannot command any one, by word of mouth, to be arrested; for he must do it by Writ, or order of the courts, *according to law;* nor may the King arrest any man for suspicion of treason or felony, as his subjects may. (2 Inst. 186.) "If the King command me," said one of the Judges to Henry VI., "to arrest a man, and I arrest him, he shall have an action of false imprisonment against me, though it were done in the King's presence."

It must be done by some order, writ, precept, or process of some of his courts. (Hale, P. C. 2, 131.) Even a mandate, under the Great Seal, is void. The Secretary of State may, however, issue a warrant in England, but he cannot seize papers. (Tom., L. D. 1, 361.) So, also, can the Privy Council, or one of them, for treason or other offences against the State; but this is by the Common Law, (Ibid.) and would not apply to the President or officers of our cabinet. The commitment should set forth the crime, with convenient certainty, even in these cases; or the court ought to bail or discharge on Habeas Corpus; and this holds good not only when no offence is specified in the warrant, but also where it is loosely set forth. (Ibid.)

The principle (B. p. 13) of exemption from discretionary imprisonment, without being allowed bail or trial, "is too perfect for human society," it is the opinion of Mr. Binney; "at least the condition human society has assumed for several centuries." He grants (p. 56) that "Discretionary imprisonment is an *ouster* from all the benefits of Government; benefits which belong to every citizen, until he is *accused* and convicted of crime."

Human society must be degenerating. The principle was, to be sure, "the occasion of fierce struggles between Kings and people in England, before Magna Charta and after." (B. p. 13.) Was this the fault of the King or the people? Is it not notorious that "the arbitrary discretion of any man is the law of tyrants? It is always unknown, it is different in different men, it is casual, and depends upon constitution, temper and passion; in the best, it is oftentimes caprice; in the worst, it is every vice, folly and passion to which human nature is liable." (De Lolme on the Eng. Con., 455.) And were not those Kings endeavoring to obtain that arbitrary discretion? Did not John sell the kingdom to the Pope? Did not Henry VIII., Mary and Elizabeth act as tyrants, and James and Charles endeavor to do the same?

It will be observed that Mr. Binney thinks that "The principle of the Common Law is not the principle of the Constitution of the United States." (P. 26.) That is, the right to be a free subject to the law. In this country there is a power which may suspend the Writ of Habeas Corpus; but it does not follow that that power may arrest or detain without oath or probable cause. The right to delay trial, discharge or bail, would not give the right to arrest, as thought by Mr. Binney. The principle of the English Constitution is, that the King, by his warrant duly authenticated, may order an arrest for suspicion, or without probable cause. The acts in England suspending the effect of the Writ, do not authorize the arrest; they delay the discharge. The right to suspend the privilege here, delays the discharge, does not authorize the arrest. English analogy as to arrest has no application. The right to arrest by warrant is a judicial act. The principle of the English Constitution, in its utmost extent, as to arrest and suspension, is not the principle of ours; it has been qualified. It needs no argument to prove that the Convention never intended to give the Executive this right. The Debates show this conclusively; and as a further evidence of the intention of the framers of this Government, and the meaning of the Constitution, attention is called to a question which arose in 1798, as to the right of the President to arrest, by warrant, persons who were aliens, under what was then popularly known as "The Alien Act." This Act provided, that the President might order all such aliens as he should deem dangerous to the peace and safety of the United States, or should have reasonable grounds to suspect were concerned in any treasonable or secret machinations against the Government,—to depart therefrom within a given time expressed in the order. Any alien found therein, after the time given, was to be, on conviction, imprisoned for a term not exceeding three years, and was never to be admitted as a citizen. The President was authorized to order to be removed out of the United States, any alien who might or should be in prison, in pursuance of the Act; and to cause to be arrested and sent therefrom such of those aliens as had been ordered to depart, and had not obtained the license specified in the first section; and if such person voluntarily returned, he was to be imprisoned, so long as, *in the opinion of the President, the public safety might require.* And the Circuit and District Courts of the United States were given cognizance of all crimes and offences against the Act. (Story's Laws, vol. 3, p. 66.) This law was intended to counteract the intrigues of the emissaries of the French Directory who were in this country, and who were trying to stir up a feeling amongst the people against the Government; and it, together with the "Sedition Law," contributed to break up and defeat the Federal party, in 1800; they also produced the celebrated Virginia Resolutions of Mr. Madison, and Kentucky Resolutions of Mr. Jefferson in favor of State Rights. In the first Resolutions, presented to the Virginia House of Delegates, December 21, 1798, the Assembly protest that the "Alien Act" exercises a power nowhere delegated to the Federal Government, which power, by uniting the Legislative and Judicial powers to those of the Executive, subverts the general principles of free government, as well as the particular organization and positive provisions of the Federal Constitution;" and in "The Address to the People" which accompanied these Resolutions, it is remarked, "This bill contains other features, still more alarming and dangerous. It dispenses with trial by jury, it violates the Judicial system, it confounds Legislative, Executive and Judicial powers; it punishes without trial, and it bestows upon the President despotic power over a numerous class of men. Will the accumulation of power so extensive in the hands of the Executive over aliens, secure to natives the blessings of republican liberty?

A lover of monarchy, who opens the treasures of corruption, by distributing emolument among devoted partisans, may, at the same time, be approaching his object, and be deluding the people with professions of republicanism. He may confound monarchy and republicanism, by the art of definition. He may varnish over the dexterity which ambition never fails to display, with the pliancy of language, the seduction of expediency, or the prejudices of the times; and he may come at length to avow, that so extensive a territory as that of the United States, can only be governed by the energies of a monarchy; that it cannot be defended except by standing armies, and cannot be united except by consolidation." (Elliott's Deb., vol. 4, p. 528, &c.) *Optimi consiliarii mortui.*

By the Kentucky Resolutions, passed November 10, 1798, after declaring "the Alien and Sedition Acts," as void and of no effect, referring to the "Alien Act," by the sixth resolution, Mr. Jefferson writes: "The same act undertaking to authorize the President to remove a person out of the United States, who is under the protection of the law, on his own suspicion, without trial by jury, without public trial, without confrontation of the witnesses against him, &c., is contrary to the Constitution, and is not law, but is utterly void, and of no force."

"The friendless alien may be selected as the safest object of the first experiment; but the citizen will soon follow. That these and successive acts of the same character, unless arrested on the threshold, may tend to drive these States into revolution and blood." (Ibid., 540, &c.) The Alien Act expired, of its own limitation, June 25th, 1800.

"By this act," said Mr. Livingston, in a speech delivered in the House of Representatives, June, 1798, "the President alone is empowered to make the law—to fix in his own mind what acts, what words, what thoughts or looks shall constitute the crime contemplated by the bill; that is, the crime of being 'suspected to be dangerous to the peace and safety of the United States.' This comes within the definition of a despotism—a union of Legislative, Executive and Judicial powers. My opinions on this subject are explicit: they are that wherever our laws manifestly infringe the Constitution under which they were made, the people ought not to hesitate which to obey. If we exceed our powers, we become tyrants, and our acts have no effect."

This law was pointed at aliens, disturbing the peace of the community, and might be very well placed under the power of removing aliens with whose nation we were at war, which is perfectly consonant to the rules of International law. This is the ground upon which it was placed by a Committee of Congress, in a Report made in February, 1799. The power conferred on the President by the Alien Act was never exercised. (Address on Madison, by John Quincy Adams.)

The Constitutionality of the Act was, therefore, never brought into question; there is, therefore, no judicial opinion on the subject; but, reasoning from analogy, no doubt should exist in our minds that the President has no right, constitutionally, to arrest and imprison citizens upon his own warrant, whether under oath or not. The Constitution of the United States was made for all time, and not as a creature of the moment; and the letters and writings of all contemporary statesmen show that rebellion and invasion were both contemplated, and that the Constitution was made for them, as well as for a state of tranquillity and peace. (*Vide* Ell. Deb., vol. iv., p. 554, &c.) These facts show, without any further remarks at present, that the Executive has not power under the first proposition. As to the second, that he has such a right, derived from the nature of the Executive office, it is necessarily included in the former; and, as there is not a word to be found in the Constitution to authorize an arrest by the Executive, he cannot have the power by virtue of his office; besides, he is "to take care that the laws be faithfully executed." (Sec. 3, Art. II.) Everything, as remarked by Mr. Binney, shows an intent to keep power from the Executive—a jealousy towards the one, a confidence in the many. The President has, therefore, no constitutional right to arrest of his own motion, under the required conditions.

2d. OF THE RIGHT OF THE PRESIDENT TO SUSPEND THE PRIVILEGE OF THE WRIT OF HABEAS CORPUS, *and to detain of his own motion, as derived from the Constitution, subject to the conditions therein specified.*

Under this we shall consider,
1. The word privilege.
2. The acts of the Convention which framed the Constitution, those which ratified it, and cotemporary exposition.
3. That the language of the clause was the customary language of the day.
4. The position of the clause.
5. The authorization of the suspension.
6. The care of the public safety.
7. That this clause requires a law to define it.
8. That the Executive is the most likely to abuse the power, without any corresponding responsibility.
9. That impeachment is not a sufficient check.
10. The decisions of the courts, and opinions of the text writers.

There are two ways of treating the question, remarks Mr. Binney; "one of them the legal and artificial, the other the constitutional and natural." We have always been brought up in the school which considers the law the perfection of reason, especially the Common Law. That the constitutional may be other than the legal, it is thought, Mr. Binney's pamphlet shows; that is, if the constitutional be admitted as different from the legal. But that the constitutional and the legal should be the same, and that the natural should not be different from either, it will be our endeavor to show hereafter. "Reason is the life of the law; nay, the common law itself is nothing but reason; which is to be understood of an artificial perfection of reason, gotten by long study, observation, and experience, and *not every man's natural reason:* for, *Nemo nascitur artifex,* (no one is born an artist.) This legal reason *est summa ratio.*" (Co. Litt., 97,—b.) *Nihil quod est contra rationem est licitum.* (Nothing against reason is lawful.) Mr. Binney is certainly too much of a correct reasoner, in general, to imply that every man's uncultivated reason is to be the exponent of the Constitution, that every man is a constitutional lawyer. "No man," says my Lord Coke, "out of his own private reason, ought to be wiser than the law, which is the perfection of reason. (Ibid.)

"Reason," says another writer, "is the soul of all law. The common law of the land is founded on reason: equity is reason perfected, unwritten, but perfecting written law.

"Statute or written laws are deductions drawn from common law, which is founded on right reason, culled and drawn from the experience of ages, and admitted as such by the consent of wise men."

It was, likely, the intent of the author to imply that the legal is the constitutional, the artificial the natural properly, trained to reason logically and legally; for, if he did not so mean, he implies that his own argument, not being the legal, must be the illegal. A thing is either legal or not legal. His argument, not being the legal, is the illegal. This it must be, certainly, if contrary to what is laid down by legal authority; and he certainly cannot mean—or if he does intend it, he is contrary to Coke, the great legal exponent of the liberty of the subject, in the days of the "murdered king,"—that the natural mode of treating the subject is contrary to the legal, for nature or natural cannot be contrary to true reason. But, owing to our imperfections, it is necessary to drill and mortify the mind, to bring it nearer to perfection. If this is a correct surmise, that Mr. Binney intends that the legal is the constitutional, and that he does not intend the illegal to be the constitutional; and that, besides this, he means, by the legal and artificial, that which has been produced by study, and is the product of the trained legal mind; and means by the natural that which is the product of the mind untrained to reason, we think he must necessarily yield to our conclusion, that his argument in the introduction is contrary to the after argument. For he says, immediately after that which has been already referred to, "In the first mode" (i. e., the legal,) "may be presented an argument against the President's power, until Congress have authorized it, *which it may not be easy to answer*, if the premises are admitted." That is the legal and artificial; and, as made out, it is thought, the constitutional and natural is not easy to answer; which implies, necessarily, that the illegal argument, being contrary to reason and law—which is the perfection of reason, and the result of the wisdom of ages—is not difficult to answer.

The question is not who is to suspend, but which is the right, the legal, the constitutional way to suspend the privilege? Who the proper power for the security of the Government, its continuance, and the safety and security of the people and their liberties?

1. *The word privilege, in this clause of the Constitution, does not mean a mere personal privilege, applying only to each man arrested.*

"Suspending the *privilege* of the Writ is not an English law expression. It was first introduced into the Constitution of the United States. The privilege is personal and individual, not local, but subsists in remedy." (B., p. 10.)

"The warrant of arrest, with the order that the party's privilege be denied for a season, is suspension under the Constitution. A temporary denial of the privilege by a single act, founded on the authority of the Constitution, is all that is necessary to suspend the privilege." (B., p. 11.)

Before proceeding further it will be necessary to examine into the meaning of the word PRIVILEGE, and ascertain from its use whether the argument on the other side be correct or not, for it is one of the premises of that argument. The expression the "Writ of Habeas Corpus," Mr. Binney thinks, (pp. 11–40,) means "being bailed, tried, or discharged," and in this sense he uses it. This is the effect of the Writ, not the privilege of the Writ. The Writ, if granted, obliges the power granting it to remand, bail, discharge, or try. This is not the Writ itself. The privilege of the Writ is the right to have it, to ask for it. The words "Writ of Habeas Corpus" form a technical legal phrase; they do not mean "bail, trial, or discharge." (See Mr. Binney, p. 9.)

The word Privilege—derived from the Latin *Privilegium*, from *priva lex*, private law—had a meaning in the Roman Civil Code, of which the English definition partakes. It is, in that, used to signify "the exemption of one individual from the operation of a law." (Mackintosh's Study of the Law of Nature, p. 50, note.) In the time of the Republic it meant a public law applying to an individual, and it might be beneficial or not. Cicero uses the word to signify a law injurious to the person who was subject to it. (Smith, Dict. Antiq. Lex., p. 500.)

An example of this kind of law may be found in Middleton's Life of Cicero. (Vol. i., p. 354.) The opinion of Cicero upon it may be found in his Oration delivered to the Senate on his return. (And see *Cic. pro Dom.*, p. 17; *pro Sextus*, p. 30.) There was also another and later meaning of the word during the Empire, that of rights or advantages—*beneficia*—granted to a certain condition or class of men, as the privileges of soldiers, parents, &c. (Adams' Rom. Antiq., pp. 27, 238. See, also, Cooper's Justinian, p. 407.)

Then there is the *Privilegium canonis* of the Ecclesiastic law—the protection of a Roman Catholic clergyman; by which any person striking him is excommunicated.

By the English law a Privilege "is defined to be a private or particular law, whereby a private person or corporation is exempted from the *rigor of the common law;* or it is *some benefit or advantage granted or allowed to any persons contrary to the course of law,* and is sometimes used for a place that hath a special immunity. It is therefore personal or real." (Jacobs' Dict.; Tom. Dict.; *Terms de la Ley.*)

It is in this sense the maxim is used, "A privilege is, as it were, a personal benefit, and dies with the person." (3 Bulstrode, 189.)

But there is another sense in which the word is used, that is, to signify "any peculiar benefit or advantage, right or immunity, not common to others of the human race—advantage, favor, benefit. Thus we speak of national privileges which we enjoy above other nations. We have ecclesiastical and religious privileges, secured by our constitutions of government; originally some public act that regarded an individual.

Writ of privilege is a writ to deliver a person from custody, when arrested on a civil suit." (Webster's Dict.) So it is "an appropriate or peculiar law or rule of right; a peculiar immunity, liberty, or franchise." (Richardson's Dict.) "Public right." (Walker's Dict.) Thus Hume writes, (Essay 2d,) "As this liberty" (that is, liberty of the Press,) "is not indulged in any other government, &c., it may very naturally give occasion to the question, How it happens that Great Britain alone enjoys this peculiar *privilege?*"

And in one of the Parliamentary Debates a speaker said Englishmen were in the habit of considering the Habeas Corpus Act "as the law which gave them *privileges* and distinction above all other nations." Throughout those Debates it seems to be used in this sense.

So Chalmers, in his Annals, (vol. i., p. 639,) referring to the Colonies, and the opinion in Pennsylvania that the Great Charter applied to its inhabitants, says he "inferred that all the inhabitants were subjects, and of course were entitled to all the *privileges* of Englishmen." And when Blackstone (vol. i.,) writes about the rights and liberties of Englishmen, he means their privileges distinct from any other nation. This is the sense which is intended in this clause of the Constitution. By the right to the Writ is meant, not a mere personal privilege. The Writ has always been considered, in England, a Writ of Right, to which every subject of the King was entitled *ex merito justitiæ.* For instance, in a Habeas Corpus, in the case of "The three Spanish Sailors," (2 Wm. Blk. Rep., p. 1234,) the Court, of which Sir William Blackstone was one, said: "These men, upon their own showing, are alien enemies and prisoners of war, and therefore are not entitled to the *privileges* of Englishmen, much less to be set at liberty on a habeas corpus." (*vide* 2 Burr, p. 765.) "The statute of Charles II.," says Mr. Henry Hallam, (Cons. Hist., vol. iii., ch. 13,) "was enacted but to cut off the abuses by which the government's lust of power, and the servile subtlety of crown lawyers, had impaired so fundamental a *privilege,*" i. e., the privilege of the Writ of Habeas Corpus.

"The habeas corpus is the *privilege* of a British subject only." (Archbold, note 37 to 3 Blk. Com., p. 138.)

So the Governor of New York, 1697, complained that not only the English, but the Dutch, were "big with the *privileges* of Englishmen and Magna Charta." (3 Bancroft, 56.)

It is evidently used in this sense, Section 2d, Art. IV., of the Constitution; and Mr. Binney evidently so uses it, (p. 40.) He says: "The privilege" (i. e., of the Writ of Habeas Corpus,) "is guarantied to all freemen generally by the Constitution; and the denial, for a season, authorized."

The word is generally used in the legal sense, signifying a personal benefit or advantage of a man or class, distinct from the rest of the community; which is the sense in which Mr. Binney generally uses it, although he does not intend to make a legal argument. The sense, however, in which it is used in the Constitution is, that it is a privilege or right to the Writ enjoyed by the citizens of the United States; and this cotemporary laws, constitutions and Bills of Rights show. Thus, says Mr. Madison, "The following principles have been held sacred, that he (a prisoner) may have the *benefit* of a writ of habeas corpus, and thus obtain his release, if wrongfully confined." (Ell. Deb., vol. iv., p. 555.)

It is undoubtedly a personal privilege in the sense that the liberty of citizens is a personal privilege because it must belong to persons, but it is not a personal privilege belonging to one individual or society of individuals, distinct from the rest of the community in which he or they live.

The endeavor is to cause a supposition that, the privilege being personal, the President need only by one act suspend the privilege as to each person; that will be sufficient. (B., p. 11.) This is the same as though it was suspended as to all who commit a particular crime, except that the party does not know till after he is arrested that the Writ is suspended as to him. If this view be correct, the suspension would be like the laws of the Emperor Caligula, which are said to have been written in small characters, and hung up on high pillars, that he might entrap the people more effectually. The law should be "a rule prescribed," not existing only in the breast of the legislator. "No *ex post facto* law shall be passed," says the Constitution. The law looks forward, not backward. To be sure, the privilege subsists in remedy; it is a remedy the imprisoned person has; but it is a Writ of Right due to every one who is a citizen of this country restrained of his liberty. It has been sometimes extended to foreigners, but only as an act of grace, not of right. Freedom is the right; so is the remedy for freedom restrained without law. They are both rights, and one has no precedence over the other. Freedom would be of little use, without the right to examine into the legality or illegality of an imprisonment. Suppose it is granted that the privilege is a personal privilege; the suspension of the privilege and the suspension of the Writ, or the right to it, are the same in the end; denying the privilege is denying the Writ.

Mr. Binney appears to grant this, (p. 20.) "It is the *manner* in which the *privilege of the Writ is overruled in England*, and which *must* be done by a Legislative Act,—by an Act of Parliament. It can be done in no other way."

We have shown that the privilege is never suspended there; it is the effect only which is suspended—the right of bail, trial, or discharge. But it may be asserted that the word privilege is intended to imply merely the right to the Writ in cases of certain crimes, and not the suspension *in toto;* that it is only in these particular crimes that it is intended the privilege shall be suspended. There is no limitation on the power to suspend; it can suspend when the right to suspend arises *in toto*, if it pleases. If so, how can it be confined to particular cases? Not a word is to be found in the Constitution authorizing a suspension only in particular cases. The word does not, within itself, contain any limitation of power. The only limitation is, when or not it is to be suspended. Not a word is said that when the suspension takes place, it is to be only in certain cases; but when the facts arise which authorize action, the suspension makes us all tenants at will of our liberty. The clause refers to a privilege of the people of the United States to a legal Writ, a privilege, therefore, existing by law, but not a privilege according to the legal definition, it guarantying such privilege to all citizens.

The reason that the Constitution reads the suspension of the privilege, it is thought, is this: if the words had been Act, a question might arise whether, if the Act was suspended, the State courts might not still have Common Law jurisdiction; the words would not be suspension of the Writ, for there is no Writ till it is issued, then it would be somewhat of an anomaly to suspend it. The proper expression is, "the privilege of the Writ." This suspends the statutory Writ, either of the United States or the State courts, and also the Common Law Writ of the State courts; it is an expression that covers all cases.

Mr. Binney thinks it impossible that it meant the general or universal privilege in the United States at large, (p. 11.) This involves two propositions. 1st. The suspension of the universal privilege. 2d. The suspension of that universal privilege in the United States at large. It is the prevalent opinion of the best legal minds in the country that, the clause of the Constitution not specifying that the privilege may be suspended in only particular offences, it may be suspended by the power having the right to suspend, in every case in which the public safety may require it, in case of a rebellion or invasion; and as to the latter position, that under the present words it applies to the United States at large, if so ordered by the power having the right to suspend. If, however, the word "where," which was originally placed in the clause by the Convention which made it, in the place of the present word "when," which was inserted by the Committee on Style and Revision, doubt might arise as to whether it could be suspended, except "where, in case of rebellion and invasion, the public safety might require it." The present position of the President is, that the Writ is suspended throughout the country, so far as political prisoners are concerned, but not that it is suspended *in toto*. If Mr. Binney be correct, it can be suspended in every case and in every place. Referring to the fact of the impossibility of a general suspension, in favor of such impossibility is cited the infinite absurdity it would lead to, involving "the very persons who should suspend the privilege," and friends as well as foes of the Government. This is correct, if a total suspension must take place throughout the country, and would follow, if the power in the Constitution requires no law to control it. But the whole always contains all parts—the greater always the less. These are axioms no one would be foolish enough to deny. If correct in this, it is perfectly optional in the power having the right to suspend *in toto*, to do so *pro tanto* as well as *in toto*. Under the clause cited, this discretion requires a law to confine it. That it did not mean to speak of two acts, one of authority and one of execution, is the point in dispute; and although great weight will be given to the opinion of the author of "The Privilege of the Writ," as a learned jurist and a profound lawyer, yet it must not be forgotten that an assertion of the fact in dispute is no argument in its favor. Sir Isaac Newton was a great astronomer, and might have asserted, from defective knowledge, that the Earth is stationary, and that the Sun moves around it; the fact should not, therefore, be admitted without investigation. It is not in opinion, but reason, that law is founded. Its words are the authority for its suspension by some power; that does not necessarily imply that the President is that power; that would be begging the question. Mr. Binney will certainly not assert that, if nothing had been said in our Constitution about it, the President would have had the right to suspend; and he also, as a constitutional lawyer, knows that nothing can be implied in the Constitution against common right or human freedom. That this clause is to be construed strictly, because derogatory to the rights of the people, of the States, and against the Common Law, (*vide* Jenkins' Centuries, p. 221;) and that, by Article IX. of the Amendments, it is specified that "The enumeration in the Constitution of certain rights shall not be construed to deny or disparage others retained by the people;" and by Article X., "That powers not delegated to the United States by the Constitution, nor prohibited by it to the States, are reserved to the States respectively, or to the people."

"The Government of the United States can claim no powers which are not granted to it by the Constitution, and the powers actually granted must be such as are expressly given, or given by necessary implication." (Martin vs. Hunter's Lessee, 1 Wheat., 304.)

The word "suspend" is derived from the Latin *sub* and *pendo*, to hang, and is defined by Webster "To interrupt, to intermit, to cause to cease for a time. To cause to cease for a time from operation or effect, as to suspend the Habeas Corpus Act." By Richardson: "To hold, to keep in doubt and uncertainty, to remove or withhold from, to withhold, to keep back for a time." By Johnson: "To interrupt, to make to stop for a time; to delay, to hinder from proceeding; to debar for a time from the execution of an office or enjoyment of a revenue."

These lexicographers also give the definition "to hang" given by Mr. Binney, but it is distinct from those above given. Webster applies one definition to the case of the privilege of the Writ. He calls it incorrectly, as Blackstone has done, suspension of the Act. The peculiar magic Mr. Binney sees in the word "suspend," it is not easy to comprehend. The word may be considered as having the same meaning as the words—deferred, delayed, abeyance, cessation, discontinuance or interruption. Its meaning "to hang," can hardly apply to the privilege of the Writ; the other words would have the effect of suspending the privilege, if they had been used. It is difficult to see that "it is the only word that could be used to give character to an Act of Congress," (B. p. 51,) deferring the privilege.

There is another reason why the word "privilege" was used. It is discretionary, to a certain extent, with a Judge, whether he will grant the Writ in the first instance or not. He requires a petition to be presented, setting forth the facts of the case, and an affidavit, and in some cases and in some courts, a rule on the attorney representing the Commonwealth, to show why the Writ should not issue. On this rule or petition and affidavit, the question is argued, or passed *sub silentio*, as to granting or not granting the Writ, and sometimes it is refused. (See Hobhouse's case, 3 Barn. & Ald. 420, 2 Burr. 765,—2 Wm. Blk. Rep. 1324, 7 Wheat. 38, 1 S. & R. 353, 3 Peters, 193, 2 How. Rep. 65, 3 Ibid. 103.) It must be first shown in the Supreme Court (U. S.) that the court has power to grant the Writ. (9 Peters', S. C. R. 704.)

Here the privilege of the Writ is to be suspended, not the effect of the Writ. In England the effect is suspended. The Writ, it has been shown, requires a petition and affidavit, from which the Judge ascertains whether to grant it or not; for although it is a Writ of Right, it is not a Writ of course. (2 Casey Penn'a Rep. 1; Williamson's case.) Thus Vaughan, C. J.: "It is granted, on motion, because it cannot be had of course; and there is, therefore, *no necessity to grant it; for the court ought to be satisfied* that the party had probable cause to be delivered." (Bushell'scase, 2 Jones, 13.)

This discretionary power in every case, it has been shown, produced the Statute of Charles II. The words "Writ of Habeas Corpus" express a known legal, therefore a technical Writ. (Mr. Binney, p. 9.)

"Where technical words are used, the technical meaning must be given them." (U. S. vs. Jones, 3 W. C. C. R. 209, Story Com. 2 Book, 5 ch. Sedw. on Cons. Law, 261.)

"If a statute makes use of a word, the meaning of which is well known, and has a definite sense at the Common Law, the word shall be expounded and received in the same sense in which it is understood at the Common Law." (Dwar. on St. 696.)

Under the Statute of 31 Charles II., there is 1st, A privilege of the person imprisoned or detained to the Writ. (Ante. p. 13.) 2d. An effect resulting from that Writ when issued. (Mr. Binney, p. 20.)

The suspension of the privilege, means a suspension of the right to the Writ, not a suspension of the effect. If the privilege of the Writ is suspended, the Judges are to be informed of the fact, so that they may not grant it. This was likely the idea of Mr. Morris, when he moved the clause as an amendment to the Judiciary Article, as will be shown hereafter. It was the Judges who were to act, but act under the law of Congress. This was the view taken by the members of the House of Representatives, 1807. "To me," remarks one of the members, "it appears that this is a proper and necessary power to be vested in the Judges—that is, the power to *issue* the Writ, to ascertain whether a person be legally or illegally confined, and that a suspension of the Writ of Habeas Corpus is, in *all cases, improper.* If a man is taken up, and is *denied an examination* before a Judge or a court, he may, although innocent, in any case, continue to suffer confinement. He may be taken up on vague suspicion, and may not have his case examined for months." (An. of 9th Cong. 2d Sess. 413.)

So another:—

"This is a measure which ought never to be proposed, unless when the country is so corrupted that we cannot trust the Judges themselves. Whenever the whole mass of society becomes contaminated, and the officers of the Judicial Court are so far corrupted as to countenance rebellion and release rebels from their confinement, it may be then time to say, they shall no longer remain in your hands; we will take them from you." (An. 9th Cong. 2d Sess. 414.)

That the issuing of the Writ by the Judges is the privilege to be suspended. (*Vide* Ibid. 530, 546, 562, 567.) This will account for Mr. Wilson's remarks in the Convention of 1787. He refers to the discretion of Judges, and deems that sufficient, without any interference on the part of Congress to control that discretion. The privilege of the Writ, is the right to ask for the Writ, upon petition and affidavit, in the first instance, from the Judges of the court—not the effect of the Writ, which is to bail, discharge, try, remand or not. The suspension of the privilege, is the suspension of the right to operate when, upon petition, the Judge is shown the crime of the party asking was contemplated by the law suspending.

Mr. Binney also says (p. 18:) "In fine, the Common Law principle requires qualification for modern times, and most of all in governments which are the least strong, and among a people who are the most free."

This is very singular reasoning; the freer the people, the less freedom should they enjoy; the man of modern times enjoys too much freedom under the Common Law,—it should, therefore, be qualified; Liberty has dug her own grave, she is *felo de se!!*

She has committed, in "the land of the free and the home of the brave," political suicide. Shades of Hampden, Selden, and of you greater than all, most dogmatical, but most noble and liberty-loving Coke, arise from your resting-place, and behold your labors blasted, your errors exposed! And ye, most noble spirits of by-gone days, More, and Sidney, and Locke, where are ye? Have ye deserted the fane of Freedom? Have we mistaken your foot-prints? Are your labors but as the cord of Ocnus, the work of Sisyphus, the endeavors of the Danaides? But as

> "Structures, rais'd by morning dreams;
> Sands, that trip the flitting streams;
> Down, that anchors in the air;
> Clouds, that paint their changes there."

Is liberty a shadow, or a beautiful fruit, to turn to ashes when it touches the lips? Has thy day arrived, most sophistical Hobbes, most subtle Machiavelli, most monarchical Filmer? Must we, at last, acknowledge that "this is the curse which waits on man's wilfulness? Of our own works we soon grow weary; to-day we worship, to-morrow we loathe them. The laws we have imposed on ourselves, knowing how baseless and strengthless they are, we are impatient to throw off, and then we are glad to bow even to a yoke of iron, if it will be but to deliver us from the misery of being our own masters."

Have not Parliament and the English people been fighting for centuries, to obtain the position which Mr. Binney tries to abolish by a stroke of the pen?

"*The Habeas Corpus Act of England, with this discretionary power of Parliament, affords no analogy for the United States,* who have qualified the principle, so as to secure it against the discretionary power of any body, *except when* the nation is forced away from its normal and orderly condition by internal war, rebellion or invasion." (B. p. 19.)

An acknowledgment is here made that the people of the United States left a discretionary power to somebody in these cases. Who has that discretionary power—the Executive or Congress? English analogy would say the latter, together with the Executive. Liberty would say the same. Law, History and cotemporary exposition are likewise. Is it not also a question, the Constitution saying that it is to be suspended on certain contingencies, when those contingencies arise, as to the manner of suspending, saying nothing to the contrary,—whether English analogy, as far as it can, is not to govern? Are we not using an English law expression, the "Writ of Habeas Corpus?" Is there not a known method of getting rid of this Writ—i. e., suspension of the privilege? Is it not customary in England to get rid of it, by suspending the effect, not repealing the Act? Have we not taken our idea of suspending the privilege from that?

"In such a condition, the Government cannot,—properly speaking, will not, and cannot extensively,—abuse the exception," says Mr. Binney; and the reason he gives is that "the exception cannot be either *usefully* or *constitutionally* applied, except to defeat a sympathy with domestic or foreign enemies, to the overthrow of the fundamental institutions of the people." This has been done before. Every record of the past, treating of the downfall of Democracies, is evidence proving the danger of trusting too much to rulers. It is true, if the exception were always usefully and constitutionally applied, there would be less danger; but where is the check upon the Executive? What is constitutionally applied? Where is the restriction in the Constitution, controlling the power of the Executive?

2. *The Acts of the Convention which framed the Constitution of the United States, of those which ratified it, the words of the State Constitutions and Bills of Rights, and of those who lived at that time, show that Congress is the power, together with the Executive, to suspend the privilege.*

The Convention which framed the Federal Constitution, began its sittings, May 14, 1787, but no business was transacted till the 28th. On the 29th, Charles Pinckney exhibited his plan, the sixth Article of which related to the Legislature, and contained the following sentence:—" The Legislature of the United States shall pass no law on the subject of religion, nor touching or abridging the liberty of the press; *nor shall the privilege of the Writ of Habeas Corpus ever be suspended,* except in case of rebellion or invasion."

This was not a new expression; the same had been used in the Constitution of Massachusetts of 1780, with the addition of some words.

Mr. Binney thinks it very probable that Mr. Pinckney intended by the expression, that the Legislature was to be the power to suspend, that he was using it in the legal sense—i. e., the customary language of the day. Three months after, on the 20th of August, 1787, about three weeks previous to the adjournment, *sine die,* of the Convention, the Writ is again mentioned by Mr. Pinckney, not as in the plan referred to already, emanating from him; but as one of a number of distinct propositions to be referred to the Committee of Detail. This time it is—" The privileges and benefits of the Writ of Habeas Corpus shall be enjoyed in this Government, in the most expeditious and ample manner; and shall not be suspended *by the Legislature* except upon the *most urgent and pressing occasions,* and for a limited time, not exceeding   months."

This would place it in the power of the Legislature to suspend the privilege on those occasions, but it would not have been identical with the power of Parliament. They can suspend in time of peace; that would not be the effect of this clause. Mr. Binney thinks that it would have given the Legislature "the omnipotent power of Parliament"—that "it would have brought the Constitution, in this respect, *into perfect identity* with the Constitution of England, with a *maximum* limitation of time, instead of the pleasure of Parliament." This he considers to have been perfectly proper, as regards the power placed in Congress. "Certainly," says he, "if the occasions of its exercise were to be *indefinite*, however urgent and pressing, as he now proposed, nothing would have exceeded the incongruity of committing such power to the Executive department of the Government." Is it not virtually as indefinite, though not expressly so, under the clause in the Constitution, if no law be required? How long will a rebellion last? How long may the public safety require its suspension? Do "urgent and pressing occasions" make it indefinite,—if so, would not the same be the case in a rebellion? Who is to judge how long it is to be suspended? The one who has the power to suspend, the one who is the judge of its necessity, the power who is to exercise it.

On the 28th of August, the subject was resumed. "Mr. Pinckney, urging the propriety of securing the benefit of the Habeas Corpus in the most ample manner, moved that it should not be suspended but on the most urgent occasions, and then only for a limited time, not exceeding twelve months."

It does not appear from this whether this was a renewal of the preceding motion or not; likely it was.

"Mr. Rutledge was for declaring the Habeas Corpus inviolate. He did not conceive that a suspension could ever be necessary at the same time in all the States."

This is somewhat vague; the first assertion is that the privilege should not be suspended, that is, if Mr. Pinckney's motion was similar to the preceding, and that the word "privilege" does not appear to have been dropped, is apparent from the motion of Mr. Morris, given hereafter. The second implies a suspension, but not in all the States at the same time, the latter part regarding the locality of the suspension, not considering the privilege as a mere personal privilege.

Mr. Binney thinks that this intends a suspension of the Writ or Act as the object, and disposes of it by declaring that Mr. Rutledge made a mistake in what he said, or that Mr. Madison made a wrong report, or that the mind of both or each of them did not embrace the *technical* doctrine on the subject. Does he forget that his theory is that no technical doctrine was intended, that he is giving in his argument a natural effect to the words, not a legal? He then says, (p. 29,) "Enough, however, is recorded to show that it must have been in the minds of the delegates under at least three aspects: 1. *Suspension of the privilege and not of the Writ or Act.* 2. Suspension by the Legislature, and only by the Legislature. 3. Suspension generally, and by the department that would be intrusted in rebellion or invasion with the safety of the public."

The first and second of these propositions go together. Those in favor of the second proposition must necessarily have judged the Legislature to be the department mentioned in the third. The first and third propositions given are contained in the clause in the Constitution—are expressed; the second proposition, which is the implied power, Mr. Binney grants was the Legislature, in the minds of the delegates, thereby giving up the whole argument in favor of Congress as far as the Convention is concerned. He also grants that the suspension would be general. The whole reads that the delegates intended suspension of the privilege generally, by the department which would be intrusted with the safety of the public in time of rebellion or invasion, that department being Congress. This will be more evident by what will be given.

As a consequence, it is likely, of the latter part of Mr. Rutledge's motion, Mr. Gouverneur Morris moved that: "The Privilege of the Writ of Habeas Corpus shall not be suspended, unless where in cases of rebellion or invasion, the public safety may require it."

Very strong ground in favor of the right of the President to suspend is thought to arise from the fact that the position in which Mr. Morris, the mover, placed it, was as an amendment to the 4th Section of the 11th Article, the Judiciary, (1 Ell. Deb. 270;) therefore, it should not be presumed that because now placed under the head of the Legislative powers, that the Legislature is the power to suspend, the change having been made by the Committee on Arrangement, which Committee had power to change the numbers and sections of the Articles, and had no power to change the import or meaning of any of them. Is not this change an evidence that that Committee judged the clause was in the wrong place? Stronger still, was it not changed by Mr. Morris, and is not this proof that he thought he had moved it in the wrong place? (*vide* Letters, 1 Ell. Deb. 507.) That the Committee did change the meaning, by the insertion of a word, has been shown.

The conclusion Mr. Binney arrives at, because the clause was originally under the head of Judiciary, that the power to suspend the Writ was not to proceed from Congress, seems rather strained. And if the intent is to govern at all, Mr. Morris having changed it from the Judiciary to the Legislative, on sober second thought, that is the place for it, and that instead of "expressly negatively, Mr. Pinckney's motion," is in its favor. Then it is said that this motion of Mr. Morris "rejected the reference to the Legislature,"—not a word is said to that effect, no debate, no word struck out, no objection, a seeming rejection by leaving out the word Legislature, which is more than balanced by what he did afterwards. When all cotemporaneous constitutions of the States, and those made immediately after, are opposed to such a construction; when Mr. Morris changed it to its present position; when all the rules of English law pointed to the Legislature; when Blackstone's Commentaries, a law book more read at the time than any other of that science, which had run through an Edition before 1774, which was commenced to be published 1771, (Washburn's Jud. His. of Mass. 196, —Burke on Conciliation,) praised the power of Parliament to suspend the Act, as one of the advantages of the British Constitution; when it is considered that English law books were imported by the colony of Massachusetts 1647, and that a book containing the Magna Charta, Habeas Corpus Act, and other English Statutes, with comments, was published in Boston, 1721; (Marvin Leg. Bib. tit. Care, Henry) when these things are considered, can it be doubted for an instant, that it was the intent of the mover and those who formed that Convention, that the Legislature was the power to suspend.

"Mr. Wilson doubted whether in any case a suspension could be necessary, as the discretion now exists with the judges, on most important cases, to keep in gaol or admit to bail." These were the remarks of a great lawyer, and there were few of his day equal to Mr. Wilson, as his Works testify. He wished the privilege to be inviolate, except as controlled by the Judges in felonies and treasons in accordance with the Statute of Charles II. He wished no suspension, and thought it was unnecessary to give such power to any one. The vote was as follows: "The first part of Mr. Gouverneur Morris's motion to the word *unless*, was agreed to *nem. con.* On the remaining part, ayes, 7; no, North Carolina, South Carolina, Georgia, 3."

The argument on the other side then proceeds on the supposition that the word Legislature being in Mr. Pinckney's original proposition, and that of Mr. Morris having been adopted in its place without it, it is to be inferred that if these propositions of Mr. Pinckney intended to confer this power upon the Legislature, the substitute disclaimed the intention by rejecting it. (B. p. 31.) This, at first sight, is a very plausible argument, but it should not be acknowledged for the reasons given, and the fact that no vote was taken on striking out the word Legislature, the proposition of Mr. Morris being a substitute for that of Mr. Pinckney, and perhaps accepted by him as such, it being more favorable to permanent liberty than his proposition, his motion being that it should be suspended on the most urgent occasions, and then but for twelve months at the utmost. This was but one suspension, and at the end of the twelve months it might have been suspended again for another period of twelve months, similar to the method in Parliament, who suspend to a certain day, and never to the next session, for the King might avoid calling a Parliament; because it was never the intent to give the Executive the power to suspend any laws; it is not, therefore, to be implied, in the absence of authority, tohim, that he is intended, especially on a matter of such vital importance, opposed to the Common Law and the liberty of the citizen; because it was always the custom in England for the Legislature to suspend the

Writ; because it never could have been the intention of those founding a Republic, to place so much power in the hands of one man as there would be in the hands of the Executive if he were the power having authority to dispense with privilege of the Writ; and also to have the right, according to Mr. Binney, to imprison at pleasure; because it was no rejection, but was merely the omission of a word not considered necessary; and because History, Law and Liberty pointed to the Legislature, as the proper power to exercise it. It cannot be presumed that "it was struck out." The reason, doubtless, that the word Legislature was disposed of, was because it was customary in England for the Legislature to suspend it, it was never for a moment thought that here the Executive would claim the power when his right was expressly negatived, and as brevity was an object, Mr. Morris probably thought, it was not necessary to insert it.

"The American Revolution," remarks a member of Congress, in a late speech, "was a protest against prerogative; it was not an assault upon the Constitution; it did not arise from dissatisfaction with its principles. It was resistance to its violations—sometimes by Parliament, much more often by the King. That revolution had been successful, and its leaders, civil and military, were come together to form a new Government. Can it be believed that they—protestants against kingly prerogative—revolutionists, because of outrages on personal rights by their sovereign—just emerged from a seven years' war in defence of those rights, and of indignant defiance of the royal tyranny—would clothe the Executive of their new Government with a power over the citizen which even their former master had never dared to pretend that he possessed? Can it be believed that they, proud of their English lineage, proud of their English liberty—aye, proud of their loyalty to the principles of the English Constitution, and fortifying themselves, at every step of the Revolution, by appeals to English example and English law—would sacrifice that right which their English ancestors accounted their chiefest glory? Those ancestors had, for six centuries, battled bravely for popular rights. They had placed the crown upon the brow of the people; they had decked it with many a jewel; it was radiant with the glories of popular liberty; and can it be believed that our fathers would tear away this priceless gem, which sparkled in the very forefront of that coronet, and with it adorn the sceptre of executive power? They speak of the Habeas Corpus as a thing existing, a privilege, whose character and extent are so engrafted upon the structure of their society and Government—a right so familiar to the minds of many; so interwoven with every theory of popular rights and executive power; so thoroughly understood—so accurately defined that it needs neither to be established nor described—a right so dearly prized that they will guard it more carefully than ever it has been guarded before; that they will establish as the very corner-stone of the new Republic, that whereas heretofore it might be suspended at the will of the Legislature, it shall hereafter be suspended by the same power only 'when, in cases of rebellion or invasion, the public safety may require it.'"

Strange indeed would have been the doings of that band, gathered to form that sacred instrument, more sacred than the Declaration—a collection of men who thought more upon the subject for which they were called together than did ever men before, and who met to form the first, the greatest, and the best Government that was ever made for the security of the rights of the people—strange would they indeed have acted had they made a Government in which they were to be tenants at will of their liberty, at every petty outbreak or disturbance; if they intended that Congress was to be prolific, as was the Fox in the fable, but that the Executive was to bring forth one, that one a Lion. The Magna Charta is nothing, without the right to examine into the legality or illegality of an imprisonment, and the right to discharge, if illegal. It is but poor comfort to the man rotting in a dungeon to behold Lazarus on Abraham's bosom. He may see the water; the cup is not for his parched lips. He may dream of flowers, and skies, and the bright sun, but they are not for him to behold. Like the blind, the beauties around him may be expatiated upon by the orator, or sung by the poet, but they are not for him to behold; the precious jewel of liberty, which is as pure and unsullied as the dew-drop in the morning's light, or the odor of the rose distilled by a summer's sun, is not for him; he may know that he is entitled to it, but the pang is none the less painful from his knowledge of that—none the more sweetened by that recollection.

But this is not the only light in which to view it. Public liberty is as essential an ingredient of civilization as public security or order. "By public liberty," says Heron, "I mean freedom of discussion, freedom of action, including absolute personal liberty, a free press, and a representative Government." (Hist. of Juris., p. 13.) This he afterwards more explicitly defines. "Liberty is freedom of action, controlled only by laws tending to promote the greatest happiness of the greatest number." (Ibid, p. 71.) It "is not an empty word, an imaginary being created by the poets, but a powerful and real benefactress of the nations. She works prodigies, multiplying a hundred-fold the forces of the imagination and the soul; stimulating the keen rivalry which she excites; offering to person and property that certainty without which there can be neither industry nor commerce; finally, making all ideas and interests converge towards the common good." (Ibid, p. 271.)

History opens to us the record of the great Past; page after page she unfolds to the view, and they confirm these assertions. Russia and Austria on the one side, England and France on the other. Look at the writers; the progress of the latter, the imbecility and inanition of the former—the frost-blight wherever they touch. And in the far distant past what do we behold? Greece, with her marble palaces and temples—that of Diana at Ephesus, of the Olympian Jupiter at Athens, of Apollo at Melitus, the Pantheon and the temple of the Delphian Apollo; her Phidias, Praxiteles, Apelles and Zeuxis, Socrates, Plato, and Aristotle—and compare her with the Persian satrapies, the Gaulish towns, the British villages. Rome, with Virgil, Horace, Cicero and Cæsar, with Greece under her control, and Rome as a debased and sunken Empire, under the Twelve Cæsars—Tiberius, Caligula, Nero; one setting fire to the city, that he might sing his poem on the destruction of Troy; another elevating his horse to the Consulate; the first indulging in the infamous debaucheries at Caprea.

Italy under the Republics; Italy under the Despot; "*Genoa la superba*," with its palaces; Venice, with her canals, her commerce, her bridges, her great arsenal, and her manufactories; Pisa, with her dome, her baptistery, her leaning tower, and the campo santo; Florence, with her two hundred woollen factories and thirty thousand workmen, eighty banks, and one hundred and seventy thousand inhabitants; with the England of that period, distracted with the Wars of the Roses and successive despotisms; France, desolated by English wars, the Jacquerie and the tyranny of the nobles. Recall to mind the names of the great men and scholars of that period, in England, France, or elsewhere; compare them with those of Dante, Petrarch, Michael Angelo, and Raphael Sanzio, the *Madonna di San Sisto*—the paintings in the Sistine Chapel—the *Divina Commedia*. Then look at the Genoa, Pisa and Florence of the present; Venice under the rule of the Austrian, a corpse of the past, the smouldering ruins of palaces and churches, of marble and of Art. Italy has been the abode of the despot, and Liberty, with a shriek, has left her as she left her Eastern and greater predecessor.

Then compare the free towns of Flanders with Feudalism and England under the reign of the Eighth Henry and Mary; and the latter with Italy under the Medici, Ariosto, Tasso, Machiavelli, Manutius Aldus, and Leonardo da Vinci; and do not let us forget the advancement in France at this period, under the mild reigns of Louis XII., Francis I., and Henry IV., the result of which, in the seventeenth century, was Corneille, Racine, Fénélon, Des Cartes and Pascal. Italy had commenced its decay in the sixteenth century, and was then sunk in obscurity; despotism reigned. England was just commencing the glory of the Elizabethan age, and Bacon, Shakspeare and Coke are names engraved upon the monument of Immortality. To use the words of Savage,

"From liberty each nobler science sprung;
A Bacon brightened, and a Spenser sung."

Perhaps it may be said these remarks are, to a certain extent, true; but some of these, and many other great men, lived under Emperors, Kings, and despotic Dukes, under whom Democratic institutions were but a name. We must not forget that the great men of these ages were the result of better; and, in some cases, the result of good Governments in their own age, where all had a chance to rise, if they did not advance political tenets contrary to those of their rulers.

It is not meant to imply from the foregoing that the name of Republic is sufficient to make great men. "Under the fair semblance of Republicanism has often been practised the most detestable tyranny, and the mild laws of a Republic have too often afforded shelter for knaves and tyrants, instead of a shield for the virtuous and oppressed." But, as a general thing, an individual has a better chance to rise under that form. The general standard of intellect is better. Every man taking part in the Government feels he should educate himself to understand it, and rise in the estimation of others. In a Despotism we have one individual managing the internal affairs of the people; no inducement presented for mental activity; no inducement for business, for the results would be at the will of another. Take the case of the Jew, in the reign of John of England; a tooth drawn daily till a payment made to the King of ten thousand marks. (Hol. Chron., vol. ii., p. 301.) Science, under such Government, must languish, energy be at a stand, and no love of country exist. Witness the Irish, the Huguenots, the Flemings.

Let us now see what was the understanding of the clause in the State Conventions. The reports are very meagre, but they are the best we have.

It would appear from the vote, Maryland voted unanimously. This is not so. Luther Martin, a delegate, voted in the negative. His letter to the Speaker of the House of Delegates of Maryland, January 27, 1788, (Ell. Deb., p. 375,) is as follows: "By the next paragraph the general government is to have the power of suspending the habeas corpus act, in cases of rebellion or invasion. As the State governments have a power of suspending the habeas corpus act in those cases, it was said there could be no reason for giving such a power to the general government, since, whenever the State which is invaded, or in which an insurrection takes place, finds its safety requires it, it will make use of that power; and it was urged that if we gave this power to the general government, it would be an engine of oppression in its hands; since, whenever a State should oppose its views, however arbitrary and unconstitutional, and refuse submission to them, the general government might declare it an act of rebellion, and, suspending the habeas corpus act, might seize upon the persons of those advocates of freedom who have had virtue and resolution enough to excite an opposition, and may imprison them, during its pleasure, in the remotest parts of the Union; so that a citizen of Georgia might be *Bastiled* in the farthest part of New Hampshire, or a citizen of New Hampshire in the farthest extreme of the South—cut off from their family, their friends, and their every connection. These considerations induced me, sir, to give my negative also to this clause."

Mr. Martin appears to have fallen into the usual error of calling the suspension of the privilege a suspension of the *Habeas Carpus Act*.

The debates in the Convention of Massachusetts may not be unimportant, considering the similarity of the language of this clause with that in their Constitution of 1780. On January 26th, 1788, the clause of the Constitution having been read, "Dr. Taylor asked why this darling privilege was not expressed in the same manner as in the Constitution of Massachusetts. * * * * * He remarked on the difference of expression, and asked why the time was not limited. Judge Dana said: The answer, in part, to the honorable gentleman must be, that the same men did not make both constitutions; that he did not see the necessity or benefit of limiting the time. Supposing it had been, as in our constitution, 'not exceeding twelve months,' yet, as our legislature can, so might *Congress*, continue the suspension of the writ from year to year. The safest and best restriction, therefore, arises from the nature of the cases in which Congress are authorized to exercise that power at all, namely, in those of rebellion or invasion. These are clear and certain terms, facts of public notoriety; and whenever these shall cease to exist, the suspension of the writ must necessarily cease to exist also. He thought the citizen had better security for his privilege of the writ of habeas corpus under the Federal than under the State constitution; for our legislature may suspend the writ as often as they judge 'the most urgent and pressing occasions' call for it.

"Judge Sumner said that this was *a restriction on Congress*, that the writ of habeas corpus should not be suspended, except in cases of rebellion or invasion. The learned judge then explained the nature of the writ. * * * * This privilege, he said, is essential to freedom, and therefore the power to suspend it is restricted. On the other hand, the State might be involved in danger; the worst enemy may lay plans to destroy us, and so artfully as to prevent any evidence against him; and might ruin the country, without the power to suspend the writ was thus given. Congress have only power to suspend the privilege to persons committed by their authority. A person committed under the authority of the States will still have a right to this writ." (Elliot's Deb., vol. ii, p. 108.)

The learned Judge doubtless means by—persons committed by the authority of Congress,—persons committed by the courts of justice established by Congress, not that Congress are to exercise this right outside of the courts, in cases of suspicion of treason, or treason, as do the Privy Council in England.

In the Convention held in New York, in 1788, Mr. Tredwell, objecting to the Constitution, on the ground that it did not reserve the powers not expressly granted to the people, said: "Can it be supposed that the wise body, whose only apology for the great ambiguity of many parts of that performance, and the total omission of some things which many esteem essential to the security of liberty, was a great desire of brevity; should so far sacrifice that great and important object as to insert a number of provisions which they esteemed totally useless? Why is it said that the privilege of the writ of habeas corpus shall not be suspended unless, in cases of rebellion or invasion, the public safety may require it? What clause in the Constitution, except this very clause itself, gives the general government a power to deprive us of that great privilege, so sacredly secured to us by our State constitutions?" (2 Ell. Deb., p. 399.) This refers to the power over the States, not over the courts established by the Constitution. Congress could certainly give and deprive their own courts of the right to issue the Writ, and an imprisonment by the United States courts would be a bar to the effect of the Writ when issued out of the State courts, unless it be that the clause secures the privilege, as well as provides for its suspension. The United States courts have a right to imprison, and no State court has a right to interfere with persons committed by competent authority of the United States.

On the same day, Mr. Lansing, doubtless incited by the remarks quoted, moved, as an amendment to Sec. 9, Art. I., "Provided, that, whenever the privilege of habeas corpus shall be suspended, such suspension shall, in no case, exceed the term of six months, or until the next meeting of Congress." This appears to have been amended to read, "that the privilege of the habeas corpus shall not, by any LAW, be suspended for a longer term than six months, or until twenty days after the meeting of the Congress next following the passing the act for such suspension." (1 Ell. Deb., 330.)

By a Bill of Rights which accompanied the above it was provided, "that every person restrained of his liberty is entitled to an inquiry into the lawfulness of such restraint, and to a removal thereof, if unlawful; and that such inquiry or removal ought not to be denied or delayed, except when, on account of public danger, the *Congress* shall suspend the privilege of the writ of habeas corpus." (Ibid., p. 328.)

In the Convention held in Virginia, in 1788, Patrick Henry said, Congress is the power to suspend the Writ, (3 Ibid., 461;) and he objected to this clause because it did not sufficiently secure the right to the Writ. "The existence of your dearest privileges," said he, "will depend on the consent of Congress." (Ibid., 462.)

This Convention appointed a committee to draft amendments to the Constitution, the 10th of which is: "That every freeman restrained of his liberty is entitled to a remedy to inquire into the lawfulness thereof, and to remove the same, if unlawful; and that such remedy ought not to be denied or delayed." (Ibid., p. 658.)

The foregoing remarks certainly prove the opinion of the people of the States of that day, that Congress was the power to suspend the privilege.

But it may be said by Mr. Binney, that since the Constitution, the President may dispense with laws, that the Constitution, so far as this clause goes, authorizes it as to this Writ. The right claimed to suspend certain laws was one of the most dangerous to the liberty of the subject of the claims of the English Monarchs, and was abolished in the reign of that arbitrary Stuart, James I., by Act of Parliament, (21 Jac. 1, c. 3,) and was permanently disposed of, on the succession of William and Mary, by the Declaration of Rights, 1688, before mentioned. The question has, however, arisen nearer home. It was proposed, on Monday, June 4th, 1787, in the Federal Convention, by Mr. Butler—after the defeat of the proposal to give the President an absolute negative on the laws—"that the resolution be altered so as to read, 'Resolved, That the national Executive have power to suspend any legislative act, for the term of ——.' Dr. Franklin seconded the motion.

"Mr. Gerry observed that the power of suspending might do all the mischief dreaded from the negative of useful laws, without checking unjust or unwise ones.

"On the question of giving this suspending power, all the States—to wit, Massachusetts, Connecticut, New York, Pennsylvania, Delaware, Maryland, Virginia, North Carolina, South Carolina, Georgia—were, No." (Madison Papers, 154.)

The refusal to give the power is a negative of it.

The Legislature is the only power to suspend legislation in a Limited Monarchy, *a fortiori* in a Republic; and, unless power to do so is given expressly by the Constitution, it is never to be presumed, especially in questions like the one we are discussing. "Statutes which take away trial by jury, and abridge the liberty of the subject, ought to receive the strictest construction." (Dwar. on Stat., p. 749.) If the above argument is correct, the only power that can suspend laws is the Legislature. In England it is the King, Lords and Commons; here, Legislature and Executive uniting, and passing a law to that effect.

Mr. Binney thinks that the people of the United States did not have a right existing by law to the Writ, at the time of the formation of the Constitution; that the word privilege did not refer to a legal privilege; it was not the intent to refer to a legal privilege, and that the word was used only to describe the right of discharge, bail, or trial, not a right by law. From this he deduces that it does not require a law to suspend it. He says, (p. 10,) "The United States, while the Constitution was in the course of formation, had no Writ of Habeas Corpus, or Habeas Corpus Act; the clause *therefore does not refer to any particular law*, statute, or writ that was *in operation or use in a particular place*. (See, also, pp. 11–40.)

Previous to the formation of the present Constitution—i. e., under the Confederation —the Writ of Habeas Corpus, issued out of the State courts, in every case of detention or commitment by either the Government of the United States, of a State, or of a State court, when the plaintiff made out such a case as the law would cover, the privilege was existing, by virtue of, and issued according to the due course of law. The rule is that a law only can repeal or suspend a law, or that which exists by law, either mediately or immediately—the privilege was, under law, existing by it. The Constitution was then made; the Convention were legislating on a privilege of the Writ of Habeas Corpus, existing by law—that was the only kind. It has been shown what the effect of this clause is (page 23;) it guarantied the privilege in all cases, with the exceptions mentioned, and in those cases it was left to be suspended by some power. Is that the Executive or Legislative power? The suspension, when it occurred, was to be of something existing by law. From the settlement of the country down to the time of a suspension, when it occurred, it was to be of that which existed by law. This contemplated a law, and a law is necessary to suspend the privilege under the Constitution. The Constitution did not oust the legal jurisdiction of the State courts; the Writ has since issued concurrently with the courts of the United States, in all cases of commitment and detention, except where a conflict of jurisdiction would arise.

Congress afterwards passed the Act of 1789. This gave power to the United States courts to issue the Writ. They had, perhaps, no power except by virtue of this Act. This did not oust the jurisdiction of the State courts; they have concurrent jurisdiction to issue Writs of Habeas Corpus. If the commitment is by a United States court, the reason a State court could not interfere would be on account of the rule that the jurisdiction of each court is supreme within its own sphere. (2 Casey, p. 17, P. R. 23, 7 W. & S. P. R., 108.) If Congress have power to repeal the Act of 1789, no Writ could issue out of the United States courts, unless there is some authority for its issuing, by the clause allowing suspension, and guarantying it in time of tranquillity. The State courts would have jurisdiction to issue the Writ, in every case of commitment. When Congress suspend the privilege, they would then suspend the Constitution or law of the State.

"It may be worthy of remark," said Marshall, C. J., (4 Cranch. 95,) "that this Act (of 1789) was passed by the first Congress of the United States, sitting under a Constitution which had declared 'that the privilege of the Writ of Habeas Corpus should not be suspended, unless when, in cases of rebellion or invasion, the public safety might require it.' Acting under the immediate influence of this injunction, they must have felt, with peculiar force, the *obligation of providing efficient means by which this great Constitutional privilege should receive life and activity; for if the means be not in existence, the privilege itself would be lost, although no law for its suspension should be enacted.* Under the impression of this obligation, they give, to all the courts, the power of awarding Writs of Habeas Corpus.

"It has been truly said, that this is a generic term, and includes every species of that Writ. To this it may be added, that when used singly—when we say the Writ of Habeas Corpus without addition, we most generally mean that great Writ which is now applied for; and, in that sense, it is used in the Constitution." The Writ here spoken of, is the Writ *ad subjiciendum*.

From these remarks of the Chief Justice, we deduce the following argument: If nothing had been said in the Constitution on the subject of the privilege of the Writ, it must be acknowledged that it would have been necessary for Congress to have made a law for the Writ to issue, before it could have been issued by the United States courts. (Ibid., An. 9th Cong., 2d Sess. 503 — 529, 541, 588, &c.) The clause in the Constitution makes no alteration of this proposition—i. e., Congress must make a law to give life to the privilege. The clause in the Constitution, Judge Marshall thinks, does not give the privilege of the Writ. Those courts were in the same position, after the Constitution was ratified, as though nothing had been said about the privilege. The Act of 1789 was then passed, giving power to issue the Writ—the privilege of the Writ. The effect of the clause may be aptly compared to a springing use; as far as it applied to those courts, it did not go into operation as to them until the making of the law, giving them power to grant the Writ. Where the privilege attached to the legal Writ existed, it went into effect immediately, and in both cases, except the conditions upon which suspension was to take place occurred, it was not to be suspended. The Habeas Corpus Act of England was a statute. The United States courts did not have the Writ by the Common Law. If this be correct, Legislation having been necessary to give the power, it existing by Legislation, and the suspension to be of the privilege in these courts as well as others, and to be of Legislation. Legislation is necessary to deprive them of the right to grant the Writ.

It is also inserted in the clause, that in all cases but those of rebellion or invasion, and the public safety requiring it, that the privilege of the Writ shall not be denied. This leaves the privilege of the Writ, in the cases of rebellion or invasion, the public safety requiring suspension, in exactly the same position as though nothing had been said in the Constitution in regard to it. The privilege is to be inviolate in other cases only; if this be so, it is optional with the power not restricted, when those cases arise. The power that has the right to give the privilege, in the United States courts, as remarked by Judge Marshall, (4 Cr. 94,) who, even where a mention of the privilege of the Writ is guaranteed by the Constitution, has, according to him, to make a law to give it vitality. It is optional with that power to restrict it; that power is the Executive and Congress; they are, therefore, the power to restrict, by law, the issuing of the Writ out of these courts, they are the suspending power.

3. *The Language of the Constitution was the customary Language of the Day.*

Mr. Binney writes, (page 7,) "But the language of the Constitution, in this particular, was not the customary language of the day, either in England or in the United States; and the Parliamentary practice was the very thing that was to be *strenuously* rejected and excluded." This involves the assertion of the following facts:

1st. That the language of the Constitution, in this particular, was not the customary language of the day.

2d. The language of the Constitution differs from the customary language of the day

3d. A customary language which differed from that in the Constitution.

4th. That, in England and the United States, the customary language differed, in this particular, from that used in the Constitution, and,

5th and lastly. That the Parliamentary practice was the thing to be excluded and *strenuously* rejected.

Then comes the statement, based on these propositions, that "the language of the Habeas Corpus clause in the Constitution was new, and is peculiar; and it must be viewed in its own light, and in the light afforded by other parts of the same Constitution."

Whether this be so, that it was intended to use the words in the Constitution in a different sense from the usual and customary, and that the Parliamentary practice was to be "strenuously rejected and excluded," is to be judged of by this argument. The burden of proof is on Mr. Binney to show this change from the usual course of things, and the usual meaning of words; especially when it has been decided that a cotemporary exposition of the Constitution fixes the construction. (Stuart vs. Laird, 1 Cranch, 299.) That there was a customary language needs no proof.

"The Constitution does not use the word *suspended* in an artificial or technical sense, for it had none in this relation." (B., p. 7.) This is true, no doubt, of the word suspended; but when the phrase is used, suspend the privilege of the Writ of Habeas Corpus, does it not become a legal expression?

By the constitution of Massachusetts, passed in 1780—seven years before the Constitution of the United States—it was provided that "the *privilege* and *benefit* of the Writ of Habeas Corpus shall be enjoyed in this commonwealth in the most free, easy, cheap, expeditious and ample manner; and shall not be suspended by the *Legislature*, except," &c. (Sec. 7, chap. vi.) And by the Declaration of Rights attached thereto "*the power of suspending laws*, or the execution of the laws, *ought never to be exercised but by the Legislature*, or by authority derived from it, to be exercised in such particular cases only as the Legislature shall expressly provide for." (Sec. 20.) The same may be found in the Declaration of Rights of New Hampshire, adopted in 1792, (Sec. 29;) also that as to Habeas Corpus, above mentioned. Also in that of Vermont, 1793, (Sec. 15;) the constitution of that State providing, "All prisoners, unless in execution or committed for capital offences, when the proof is evident or presumption great, are declared bailable."

By the Bill of Rights of Kentucky, adopted in 1799, (Sec. 16,) "no power of suspending laws shall be exercised unless by the General Assembly or its authority. (Sec. 18.) That all *persons shall be bailable* by sufficient securities, unless for capital offences, when the proof is evident or presumption great; and the *privilege of the Writ of Habeas Corpus* shall not be suspended, unless when, in cases of rebellion or invasion, the public safety may require it." And in the constitution of Georgia, adopted in 1798, (Sec. 9, Art. IV.,) "The Writ of Habeas Corpus shall not be suspended, unless when, in cases of rebellion or invasion, the public safety may require it." And in the Bill of Rights of Virginia, June 12, 1776, (Code of Virginia, p. 32,) it is written, "*That all power of suspending laws, or the execution of laws, by any authority, without consent of the representatives of the people*, is injurious to their rights, and ought not to be exercised." These quotations also prove that the word PRIVILEGE was not used to mean a mere personal privilege, as used in the law, but a privilege or benefit, or as one of the immunities or liberties of the citizens of the United States.

"We have taken from the statute book of the country the most valuable part of our Constitution," said a member of Congress, in 1807. (*Vide* An. of 9th Con., 2d Sess.) "The Convention which framed the Constitution, believing that there might be cases when it would be necessary to vest a discretionary power in the Executive, have constituted the *Legislature* the judges of this necessity." (Ibid., 422.)

"Such is the value of this privilege," remarked another, "that even the highest legislative body of the Union—the legitimate Representatives of the nation—are not entrusted with the guardianship of it, or suffered to lay their hands upon it, unless when, in cases of extreme danger, the public safety shall make it necessary." (An. of 9th Cong., 2d Sess., 502.)

"In vain does the law proclaim that no man shall be imprisoned contrary to law, if the party imprisoned has no access to a tribunal to decide the question of legality. In vain does the law promise a trial by peers, if the imprisoned party can have no access to a tribunal where he can demand such a right. In short, without the Writ of Habeas Corpus, rights of personal liberty, however solemnly proclaimed, would exist but in name. This Writ of Habeas Corpus is coeval with the rights which it secures." (J. M. Broom, of Del., An. of 9th Cong., 2d Sess., 505.)

"Great attention," remarks Mr. Dwarris, in his able work on Statutes, (page 693,) "should be paid to the views of those who lived about the time that the law was made." From Mr. Binney's remarks one might be almost led to suppose the normal condition of the people of this country is imprisonment, the abnormal freedom from arrest and detainer.

4. *The position shows that Congress should join in the suspension.*

The position of the clause under consideration is in the Article of the Constitution which treats of the Legislative power, and in the Section of that Article which restricts the powers of Congress. We can reasonably argue from this, that Congress is the power restricted—Congress is the power to suspend, when those restrictions do not apply. Mr. Binney says that the clause was placed in this section by the Committee, because it is merely a restrictive clause, not because it refers to Congress. They "placed it in the ninth section of the first article of the Constitution, which is restrictive from beginning to end." (B., p. 32.) Is not this an evidence of the intent of the makers of the Constitution, who did not object to the alteration, and of Mr. Gouverneur Morris, who proposed it, and who was the person to whom the Committee on Style left the performance of most of their labors, that he and they considered that it was in the wrong place before, and therefore he and they changed it to its proper place? Mr. Binney thinks it was placed there "for the reason, probably, that the clause is directly restrictive." This probability is afterwards advanced to a certainty; for, in referring to the XI. and XII. Amendments to the Constitution, it is remarked: "One of these was intended to abridge the judicial power, the other to alter the mode of electing the President. The whole must have the same meaning, wherever they may be placed. *Their most natural position is in the same section with the Habeas Corpus clause, as they are uniformly restrictive.*" (B., p. 34.) And, as a further argument in favor of his position, he says, (p. 33:) "With the exception of this clause and one that precedes it, and prohibits the *prohibition* by Congress of the importation of slaves prior to 1808, there is not a paragraph in the section which does not begin with a restraining and disabling *No*. Most of these paragraphs restrain and disable Congress. One of them restrains the Executive department; another of them restrains all persons who hold an office of trust or profit under the United States, in whatever department." But are not the words "shall not be suspended" synonymous with saying, no "privilege of the Writ of Habeas Corpus" shall be suspended? Is not the expression in the clause a negative?

Every clause of Sec. 9th, Art. I., applies to Congress, undoubtedly; one is, it is true, a restriction on the purse of the Executive. Congress is the power to grant or not; a restriction is placed on persons as to receiving presents, &c.; Congress is the power to withhold or waive it. These appear to be stuck in at the end of the section. The first six clauses undoubtedly apply to Congress. The whole of the Article, (forty-eight clauses,) except one clause, applies to the Legislative branch. In the first clause "the general negative of these restrictions is qualified by an express limited affirmation of the power of Congress, and there is a limited affirmation which qualifies the general negative in the Habeas Corpus clause; but with this remarkable difference, that, while the power of *Congress* is expressly affirmed in the first, it is not expressly affirmed in the second. The word *Congress* is not there." (Ibid.) Yet Mr. Binney would not argue that, if the word Congress had been left out of the first clause of this section, if it had read, "The migration or importation of such persons as any States now existing shall think proper to admit, shall not be prohibited, prior,"&c., that the absence of the word Congress would have given the Executive power to prohibit, after the period had elapsed, without any Act of Congress, or to have imposed a tax not exceeding ten dollars per man. Then how can he imply, because the word was inserted in the former clause of the same section—which is prohibitory throughout, and which, it is thought, has been already shown, was intended to apply to Congress in general—that it is not intended to apply to the next? The clause would read—the section not having been divided into numbered clauses, by the Convention—as one section. "The migration, &c., shall not be prohibited by Congress, &c.; the privilege of the Writ of Habeas Corpus shall not be suspended" by *Congress;* no bill of attainder, &c., shall be passed" by Congress; and so through the remaining clauses of the section. The first clause does not say who shall impose the tax, yet Congress would be the power. Five succeeding clauses have not the word Congress in them; in the seventh, no title of nobility is to be "granted by the United States." If Mr. Binney's argument is correct, this applies to the President. Congress is not named, therefore Congress can grant titles of nobility.

Let any one read this section, and he will agree with us, that the arguer must be in great straits who resorts to such suppositions. Is the Executive to make a bill of attainder, and pass *ex post facto* laws? Is he to lay taxes? Congress is not mentioned, except in the 1st and 7th clause. The latter says that "No person, holding office under *them* (the United States) shall, without the consent of Congress, accept any present," &c. Congress is not excluded, because not expressly mentioned in the other clauses.

That this is the restrictive clause, is hardly proved by an examination of the Constitution. That Congress shall have power to declare the punishment of treason, determine the time of choosing electors, make needful rules for territories, &c., are restrictions on the power of the people of the States, on the States, and on the Executive. They are not in section 9th.

The matter of arrangement had less consideration than any other subject. It was done by the Committee appointed to revise the style and arrangement, remarks Mr. Binney (p. 34,) yet he says that "The Committee on Style and Arrangement was the best possible." This remark is qualified, because, "though several amendments to parts of their report were offered in the Convention, no articulate consideration was given to the order and position of the different sections and clauses, as reported by the Committee. From the manner in which the amendments were made to the Constitution after it was adopted, all but the 11th and 12th have no position at all." Might not this have resulted from the fact that the Convention was satisfied that the arrangement was the best possible, as well as that the Committee was the best possible?

After the Committee made their report, September 12, the Convention was, until September 17, making amendments to that report. (1 Ell. Deb., 298.) As to those made after the adoption of the Constitution, neither the Convention or the Committee had anything to do with them.

"The Constitution has, for obvious reasons, *enumerated and specified* the powers of Congress. If Congress was to have the power of suspending the Writ, why not specify it with the other powers in the eighth section?" is asked in a triumphant way. (B. 50.) They have done so, not expressly, but by implication. By the 18th clause, (as it is now called. Originally the clauses were not numbered or headed.) Section 8th, Article I. of the Constitution: "Congress are *to make all laws* which shall be necessary and proper *for carrying into execution all powers vested by this Constitution in the Government of the United States, or any department or officer thereof.*" Under this, Congress is to make the laws to carry into execution the power of the President; though the President have the right to suspend, such a law would be both "necessary and proper," or we would be living under the arbitrary sway of one man. Mr. Binney says that the "power is vested in the President by general terms;" the power should be, therefore, made concise and clear by Congress. He thinks (p. 51) that "the law must be necessary and proper, and it is *neither when the Constitution is the law.*" Chief Justice Marshall does not agree with him. (*vide* 4 Cranch. 75.)

The Constitution is not explicit upon every point; laws are required to make it so; and we have shown that the clause we are discussing, is less explicit than most others; and also that it is the most important clause relating to our liberties in the whole of that instrument.

Every statute should be construed by the words of the statute; but where the statute is silent, we must be governed by contemporaneous exposition and by history; and that is the case with this clause, and English law giving us the Writ, and English common and statute law governing us, to a very great extent. Our Government being founded on English analogy, we should, in every case adapted to our circumstances,—and it certainly cannot be pretended that if Congress had the power to suspend, it would not be adapted to our circumstances,—we are bound to presume, nothing being to the contrary in our own law or history, that English analogy is to govern. As to the origination of the Act of Charles from jealousy of the King, it shows there must have been cause.

5. *The suspension of the privilege is not only by the Constitution, but by the power having the right to say that it shall be suspended.*

"The Constitution does not *authorize* any department of the Government to *authorize* it. The Constitution itself authorizes it." (B. p. 11, *vide* p. 21—40.) It does not authorize any department to "authorize it." This is the question in dispute—Does it authorize or empower the President, or some other department, to authorize, or does it go into effect without any authorization? Because an instrument authorizes or empowers a person to have a thing done, under certain conditions, which are to be judged of by him, that when those conditions arise, he does not authorize it to be done, is difficult to understand,—the clause in the Constitution is a double authority?

The Constitution authorizes, 1st. Some power to suspend. 2d. It also authorizes the suspension to take place when the power says it should. The privilege may be suspended: somebody is to suspend.

These distinctions the reader will bear in mind. A corollary from these propositions is, that the power authorizes the suspension. The Constitution says you are to authorize the suspension. Power is given by the people, through the Constitution, to this power to authorize this suspension. The Constitution does not authorize the suspension of the Writ, till the power to act gives the clause vitality and life—till that power says, let the Writ be suspended—then the Constitution says the Writ is to be suspended. The power saying the Writ is to be suspended, authorizes its suspension. If the power did not say, suspend the privilege, the words of the Constitution would be dead; that power authorizing gives life to the words of the instrument. There is an authority to the power to authorize, and the Constitution is an authorization of that power—it is a double authority.

It certainly will not be pretended, that a rebellion *ipso facto* suspends the privilege; yet the argument goes to that extent. The Executive, if the proper power, suspends the privilege of the Writ. He does so, because he is authorized to do so by the Constitution; he, judging from the fact of rebellion or invasion, and the public safety requiring it, does what?—Authorizes the courts to suspend the privilege. It is an Executive authorization, as well as a Constitutional. If we grant, the Executive may suspend. If the clause does not, by its necessary implication, give power to any department to authorize the suspension of the privilege, where is the right of the President to authorize the suspension, as it has been claimed he has? Are not the facts of rebellion and invasion, and the public safety, precedent conditions to suspension? Does not the department or departments, ascertaining the facts and having the power to suspend, authorize it? The Constitution empowers a power to suspend, under contingencies. When they happen, that power authorizes suspension.

We next have it asserted that "the suspension of the privilege under this constitutional power, becomes an executive act, and not a legislative act." (B. p. 46.)

This is the question in dispute; let us see how the conclusion is arrived at. We must bear in mind the argument just made, because it is upon this Mr. Binney arrives at this conclusion, and strange is the reasoning: "A power by the Constitution to authorize the suspension of a privilege, would be a power to authorize it by legislation, and then the suspension will be an executive act, under the legislative authority. The Constitution authorizes the suspension, under conditions, and therefore the suspension, in the cases supposed, is an Executive Act." (Ibid.)

We now see the object of the former argument. It was the same as saying, 1st. The Constitution authorized the suspension of the privilege of the Writ. 2d. It authorizes no one to exercise any authority in suspending; it gives no power to authorize to another; it is the only authority; therefore, the Executive is the only proper person. Let us again look at the words of the clause, lest we be led astray by the *Mutiana cautio* of Mr. Binney. The words of the clause are, "shall not be suspended, unless," &c. This certainly implies a power to suspend; it is the same as saying, "The privilege of the Writ shall be suspended," in the future, in the excepted cases, by the power having the right to suspend. This implies, 1st, A power to suspend which is not named. 2. An authority to suspend by that power, the conditional facts having been first ascertained. 3. A suspension of the privilege, under those facts. 4. A power which authorizes each suspension. The power to suspend is not mentioned. We then bring into effect Art. 1, Sec. VIII., clause 18th, vesting in Congress the right to make laws necessary to carry into execution "all powers vested by the Constitution in the Government of the United States, or any department or officer thereof." The power, therefore, belongs to Congress.

There is another kind of a power, a legal power with which this power appears to be blended by Mr. Binney.

An authority by virtue of a power of this kind is considered as the act of the original maker of the power,—it refers to real and personal estate, and cannot be delegated,—it is created by will or deed. (Sugden on Powers, 331.) That can hardly be considered this case; authority under the Constitution is delegated every day, the Constitution establishes the Legislature and the Executive, they establish the Courts; some one may say this is by virtue of the Constitution, but do they not authorize some one to execute their process? Do they not authorize it to issue—the Marshall to serve it? The Constitution authorizes many acts, but do not persons authorize those acts to be done, and so give the Constitution life, vitality?

The power of suspension being given by a written Constitution, and being qualified in it, "in regard, therefore, to the qualified right of being exempt from imprisonment without trial, *unless in cases of rebellion or invasion, when the public safety requires such imprisonment*, we must discard English analogy." (B. p. 21.) By this sentence Mr. Binney has narrowed the question down to its proper shape,—arrest is not mentioned. Must we discard English analogy in the excepted cases, nothing being in the Constitution on the subject? He says, in these excepted cases, (unless, &c.,) we must not discard English analogy, in the cases not excepted we are to discard it, in all other cases we are to accept it; this is what the writer has been trying to prove.

This is the only question that admits of argument in the clause. The Constitution of this country, it is true, as he remarks, (p. 21,) must be judged by its own distribution and ordination of powers, but certainly, we are not confined only to the jealousies or confidences which appear in it. History can be accepted as some guide to the present, especially where it is applied to an important power, the party to exercise which is not expressed, so as to ascertain who that party is.

6. *The care of the public safety is not under the exclusive control of the President, it is with Congress and the President.*

"The whole question of deciding with anthority, when in cases of rebellion or invasion, the public safety requires the suspension of the personal privilege of the Writ of Habeas Corpus, is left by this clause to the person, body, or power, invested by other parts of the Constitution, with the care of the public safety, to this intent and effect, in time of rebellion or invasion. There can be no reasonable doubt about this." (B. p. 31.)

Although the clause referred to does not point to any particular power to suspend the privilege, yet it may be reasonably argued from its wording, that the power charged with the care of the public safety is the one to suspend. The requirement is not only rebellion or invasion, which are facts, but a deduction from those facts, a result which requires thought and deliberation to ascertain—that is, the public safety. There is nothing expressed in the Federal Constitution as to who is to take care of the public safety; but the uniform custom has been to consider no particular department as charged with it, but to consider that it is a function of all the departments united, unless Congress, by law, give the Executive the power, as has been done in certain cases. The Constitution would seem to imply from the powers given to Congress, in Section 8, of Article 1, that it is the department especially charged with its care. For instance, they are to define and punish piracies, felonies committed on the high seas, and offences against the law of nations; to declare war, &c.; to raise and support armies; to provide and maintain a navy; to make rules for the government and regulation of the land and naval forces; to *provide for calling forth the militia to execute the laws of the Union*, suppress insurrections, and repel invasions; to provide for organising, arming and disciplining the militia, and for governing such parts of them as may be employed in the service of the United States; to exercise jurisdiction over all forts, dock-yards, &c., and by Section 3, Article III., they are to declare the punishment of treason. Everything in it implies that Congress is to say what the public safety requires. There is also another reason, which shows Congress should be a component department in deciding what the public safety requires.

Congress is a deliberative body, the President the power to execute the will of that deliberative body; and in every good Government there is a power to think and a power to act. A number of men think better as a mass than one; one executes the will of that number better than many. This is seen in all Republican Governments and Limited Monarchies: the Archons and the Senate, the Consul and the Senate, the Doge and the Council of Ten, the King and the Parliament, and the President and Congress;—the one to execute, the other to deliberate—to say what is to be done—executed—when the law shall be made, or when repealed or suspended *in toto* or *pro tanto:* the other to execute the result of their deliberations. Even the Porte has its Divan. The fact of what the public safety requires, is for Congress; but not Congress alone—Congress act with the President.

Mr. Binney grants the authority of the Legislature to watch over the public safety, (p. 41,) saying that "the authority of the Legislature to provide by law for the general safety of the nation, will not be brought into question." The effect of this, it is his intention to do away with, as far as it applies to the clause under consideration, by declaring that "the conditions under which this privilege may be denied, *are peculiar,* and demand consideration." These conditions are two: 1st. Rebellion. 2d. The public safety—i. e., the public safety requires the suspension. "It is not," it is said, "the *public safety in general,* but public safety in *that conjuncture of rebellion* that is referred to in the Constitution; for the clause has connected inseparably the suspension with rebellion. Rebellion and the suspension of the privilege are contemporaneous and conterraneous." We would say, in answer, is not the general safety of the public in time of rebellion the fact referred to? Does it oust the jurisdiction of Congress to watch over and attend to the public safety in the time of peace, because a rebellion occurs which demands from them increased vigilance? Because rebellion, and the privilege to be temporarily suspended, are to operate in the same country at the same time? Because connected in cause and consequence? Is that a reason to debar Congress of this power? Because they have a necessary relation, as said on the same page, will that oust the power which, it is granted, the Legislature have in time of peace, just as the power to watch over the public safety comes into full activity?

Mr. Binney thinks the President is the power to watch over the public safety, because he is,

1st. To see that the laws be faithfully executed. That clause is merely confirmatory of the Executive power; it does not give the President the right of dispensing with laws. The right to do this would make his discretion the law.

2d. To defend and protect the Constitution, and support it. It cannot be deduced from this that he is to do away with that part he considers unnecessary, for he might, at some time, under such a plea, do away with the whole.

3d. Because we have the continued voice of the Legislature, and the law, for sixty-five years, that he is both to decide the fact of the rebellion and to measure the danger to the public arising from it, and that it is his duty. The power to do this is not granted by Congress to him, but is assumed by it to be both his power and duty; and very large power is given to him on that hypothesis, to assist in the execution of what is manifestly a Legislative power, the calling forth of the Militia. It was the assumption of the first Legislature which provided for calling forth the Militia to repel invasion or suppress insurrection. It was also assumed by Congress that it was the President's power and duty to say what the public safety required, both in rebellion and invasion. (*Vide* B., p. 42.)

Mr. Binney grants that this was not the opinion of the Congress of 1792, (B., p. 43,) and mentions an example which is against his theory of the discretionary power of the Executive. It is disposed of, however, as "an absurd provision." It shows, it cannot be denied, the intent of the second Congress under the Constitution. The Act of 1792 was passed only one year after the ratification of the amendments to the Constitution, when those were living who were parties to the Constitution; when the President, who approved the Act, was George Washington, President of the Convention of 1787; when many who were delegates to that Convention were members of that Congress, (in the first Congress there were sixteen of the thirty-nine who signed the Constitution;) when the very part Mr. Binney objects to (B., p. 43, &c.,) was put in as an amendment. Antagonism to Washington, Mr. Binney says, carried the amendment, yet that existed when the Act of 1795 was passed, in which, he remarks, "insurrection and invasion were placed, in respect to the President's decision, on the same footing," (Ibid.,) in which it is assumed that it belongs to his office to decide each of these facts,—i. e., rebellion and the public safety. The Act of 1792 was to be "in force two years, and from thence to the end of the next session of Congress, and no longer." (1 Story L. of U. S., 286.) That was until two years after May 2, 1792, and the end of the next Congress, which was the Congress which met on the 3d of November, 1794, and ended on the 3d of March, 1795. So we find another Act, November 29th, 1794, authorizing the President to call out the Militia in the Western Counties of Pennsylvania. President Washington, although the President of the Constitutional Convention, never presumed, for an instant, to call out the Militia without an Act of Congress.

The only clear case, according to this Act, in which the President has been invested with discretionary power to watch over the public safety, is when "the United States shall be invaded, or be in imminent danger of invasion, from any *foreign nation* or Indian tribe." Even this it was necessary should be first authorized by a law of Congress. With regard to the right of the President to act when the public safety may require it, and take official notice of the fact, how can he go further than the clause in the Constitution which provides that "he shall take care that the laws be faithfully executed." Is the denying them, or the abolishment of them, or the suspending them, or acting contrary to them, consistent with the Constitution, and is such power given by the Habeas Corpus clause?

The opinion of Congress has been shown by these remarks, testified by their statutes; that from these statutes it cannot be presumed the President was to call out the Militia, in case of rebellion, without further knowledge of the fact than that knowledge given to every man, that by the first statute, a notification was to be given him judicially; by the next he was authorized to call out certain troops; and that, by the present Act such judicial notification is first necessary.

A word as to the constitutionality of the provisions of these Acts, which Mr. Binney (page 43) appears to doubt. Chief Justice Taney, in the case of Luther vs. Borden, (7 How. Rep., 43,) among other remarks as to the discretionary power of the President, referring to the power of Congress to control this discretion, especially as regards Section 1st of the last mentioned Act, says:

"They might, if they had deemed it most advisable so to do, have placed it in the power of a court to decide when the contingency had happened which required the Federal Government to interfere."

In a reply to Patrick Henry, by Mr. Nicholas, in the Virginia Convention, met to ratify the Constitution—Mr. Henry having objected to the Constitution on the ground that it did not declare that the civil power was to be first exhausted before the military was called upon to execute the laws of the Union, said: "From this argument it might be inferred that the executive magistrate here was to have the power of calling forth the Militia. What is the idea of those gentlemen who heard his argument? Is it not that the President is to have the power? No, sir; the President is not to have this power. God forbid we should ever see a public man in this country who should have this power. Congress only have the power of calling forth Militia. I will trust Congress, because they will be actuated by motives of fellow-feeling. They can make no regulations but what will affect themselves, their friends and relations. But I would not trust a prince, whose ambition and private views would be the guide of his actions. When the Government is carried on by representatives, and persons of my own choice, whom I can follow when far removed, who can be displaced at short periods, I can safely confide the power to them." (Ell. Deb., vol. iii., p. 392.)

From the facts we have given, Mr. Binney arrives at the conclusion that "*the perfectly untrammelled judgment of the President has been resorted to by Congress*, not by their own Legislative prescription, *but under the Constitution*, to estimate the dangers of insurrection in all degrees of force up to rebellion, and to estimate the military forces which safety requires." (Page 45.)

The contrary has been shown. The President should be informed by the Marshal and Judge that the laws cannot be executed, before he can act or take notice of the rebellion. This is granted by Mr. Binney, (p. 46.) He there tells us that "it is a breach of the President's duty, not to declare the fact, when the laws are opposed, and the execution of the *laws is obstructed by combinations too powerful to be suppressed by the usual course of judicial proceedings and the Marshal's posse.*"

This quotation of Mr. Binney's is qualified by the assertion that "the President does not decide the facts conclusively upon Congress, so as to command the means, or so that Congress must follow him by providing the means; but *he decides them officially.*" Then comes the curious assertion that this power of deciding officially is "*all that is necessary to give effect to a warrant of arrest by him, and a temporary denial of the privilege of the Writ of Habeas Corpus.*" The power of arrest is here given as a corollary from the above remarks. The President can not only stop the return to the Writ, but from suspending the right to the Writ, it is singular to say, deduced that he has the right to issue a warrant of arrest, forgetting that the V. Amendment provides that "no person shall be deprived of life, liberty or property, without *due process of law;*" that is, judicial process, which is the undoubted meaning of the phrase. The expression also means the same as "by the law of the land," in Magna Charta. (2 Coke's Inst., 50; 6 Barr., 89.) "There is no necessity for supposing, in regard to the *safety of the Country*, generally and at large, *the great measures which are to express the wisdom of the Legislature in providing for the stability and security of the Country*, and for the extension of its power, to make it safe against both Invasion and Rebellion, that these measures *are not to come from the Legislature. They are Legislative measures, and must come from the Legislature alone;* though when they are consummate as laws, they must fall within the Executive department in every particular in which that department has anything to do with them, *by force of the laws or the Constitution.*" (B., p. 45.) This is the view of the writer.

In the next sentence a curious distinction is given in regard to the law, before there is any necessity for applying it, and the effect of it at the time its application is necessary. When there is no invasion and no rebellion, then the measures for the security of the country the Legislature are to decide; they are to say what the public safety requires. "But in the case of *actual* rebellion and *actual* invasion, *the declaration or proclamation of the facts is not Legislative, but executive; and so is the decision of what the public safety requires*, for that is a conclusion of fact from other facts within the range of the same Executive duty."

Now it must not be forgotten that the Act of Congress under which the present Executive called out the three months' volunteers, is—"Whenever the *laws* of the United States shall be *opposed*, or the execution thereof *obstructed*, in any State, by combinations too powerful to be suppressed by the ordinary course of *judicial proceedings*, or by the *powers vested in the marshals by this act, it shall be lawful for the President* of the United States, *to call forth the militia* of such State or States, as may be necessary to suppress such combinations, and to cause the laws to be faithfully executed."

Now, if the Executive has discretionary power, why pass this Act with a clause which reads, the President is not to act till the laws cannot be carried out, and which impliedly says he must have notice of the fact? Did not the Congress which met after President Lincoln's call for the three months' men in April last, cure the effect of this discretion exercised by him in calling them out? Was it not deemed necessary? How can it be asserted, as on pages 43 and 44, that this Act assumes that it belongs to the President's office to decide the facts of the rebellion and the requirement of the public safety, $i.\ e.$, assumes discretion to be in him?

Why vest the President with powers under this Act, after first the "judicial proceedings" are unable to suppress such unlawful combinations, and after "the marshals" shall have exhausted the power of a sheriff which is given to them by it, either by the *posse comitatus* or otherwise? "The President," said Daniel Webster, (Address, Oct. 1832, Worcester, Mass.,) "has no authority to employ military force till he shall be duly required so to do by law and the civil authorities. His duty is to cause the laws to be executed. His duty is to support the civil authority; his duty is, if the laws be resisted, to employ the military, if necessary, but to *do all this in compliance only with law and the decisions of the tribunals.*"

"The President is to judge of the extent and necessity of the means of acting, the army, navy, and militia, and their numbers, &c.; Congress have no right to judge in this matter: if they "were to take from him the power of deciding upon the extent and necessity of these means, *it would invade the Executive Department*, which is to sustain the execution of the laws. And if they were to deny him the means, the responsibility would be with Congress." (B., p. 45.) They are to obey the behests of the President as far as these matters are concerned; according to Mr. Binney, the Executive says—I want 1,000,000 men; Congress must give them; they are not to judge of the extent of the means, or whether necessary or not; "their numbers, duration, and support, must depend upon Congress;" Congress must not refuse to give the numbers the Executive may require, or they "would invade the Executive Department."

We have shown that they have given discretionary power to Executive in certain cases, but the power came from Congress, not directly from the Constitution; that Congress had originally, in every case, jurisdiction over the Army, Navy, and Militia, the Constitution shows conclusively; if the President has power to judge whether necessary to call out the Militia, &c., he has it under the law of Congress, not directly from the Constitution.

The Executive, in case of rebellion, cannot constitutionally oust Congress of those powers it is to exercise in time of peace; those powers it is granted are at that time to watch over the public safety. Rebellion or invasion do not release the Executive from his duty to faithfully execute the laws, and he acts on his discretion, under the Act of Congress, if one be made which covers the case: when that is not controlled, as in the First Section of the Act above cited; but no one will pretend that Congress might not oblige him to act under the absurd provision referred to, (B. p. 43,) attached to the Act of 1792, if they should consider it necessary; that part of the Act was never considered to be unconstitutional, it may have been useless. That the decision of what the public safety requires, if vested in one man, is dangerous in the extreme, no thoughtful man will deny; no two men think alike, and it will not be for an instant pretended that less danger would result by allowing one to say what the public safety might require than many. "*Where no counsel is, the people fall: but in the multitude of counsellors there is safety.*" Prov. ii. 14. "Without counsel, purposes are disappointed: but in the multitude of counsellors they are established." Prov. xv. 22.

Mr. Binney thinks that these remarks meet the objection, "that any of the conditions previous to suspension require legislation in the exercise of the power of the Legislature, except as to the means, the fact of rebellion and what the public safety requires for its suppression, are of Executive cognizance and decision, and of execution also, to the whole extent of the *lawful means* of that department." (p. 46.)

In other words, the Legislature have the right to provide the means, to lay the taxes, provide the necessary number of troops or leave that to the Executive, but they have no right to say whether a rebellion exists or does not, whether the public safety requires a suspension of the privilege of the Writ or does not; yet by not giving the President power to call forth troops, by not giving the President the money from taxation, by not assisting the President in putting down a rebellion which that officer might at any time be instrumental in raising, that official may consider it necessary for the interests of the Government to imprison the whole of Congress, to be kept without bail or mainprize, *Durante beneplacito*. But there is another reason given for the power to be in the hands of the President in time of rebellion, it might be called "*Argumentum ad ignorantium.*"—An argument founded on the ignorance of the reader. The facts are advanced under which a Nation labors in case of a rebellion, and are advanced, (B., p. 47,) to prove that the President should suspend the privilege of the Writ; such a state of affairs may happen, may be in existence now; this does advance the argument in favor of giving power to the Executive; the question in giving this power is to give it to the one least likely to abuse it; the knowledge of who that should be, we derive from history, from the experience of other Governments; that power should not be the "one-man power," but the legislative should join with it, all the powers of Government acting unitedly. The Constitution has provided for the very emergencies stated.

By Art. II., Sec. 3, of the Constitution, "He, (the President,) shall, from time to time, give to Congress information of the state of the Union, and recommend to their consideration such measures as he shall judge necessary and expedient; *he may, on extraordinary occasions, convene both houses, or either of them.*" This was no doubt intended to meet a crisis like that through which we have just passed, and was acted on at that time by the President; beside, legal arrests can always be made according to the words of the Constitution, "upon probable cause, supported by oath or affirmation;" and if, upon the arrest, a Writ of Habeas Corpus is sued out, and upon the return of the Writ "it manifestly appears that no such crime has been committed, or that the suspicion entertained of the prisoner was wholly groundless, *in such cases only* is it lawful totally to discharge him. *Otherwise he must either be committed to prison or give bail,*" and in some instances is not allowed to give bail. Congress, when they meet, can suspend the privilege of the Writ. Mr. Binney also thinks: "All that is claimed for Congress to do, is upon some judgment of the facts which constitute the danger to the public, to commit the discretion to the Executive." This is hardly the fact; the discretion to detain is never given in England to the King alone, neither would it be so given here; that discretion is to be curtailed; it is to apply to some cases, not to all; it requires a warrant under oath, and a statement perhaps, to be filed by the United States District Attorney; it may be a suspension but for a temporary period, as is usual in England, or in a certain place; it may be necessary, and indeed, there always should be inserted, a saving of the privileges of the members of both Houses from the effects of the suspension during their session, unless the consent of each as to its members should be first obtained, and there are a thousand reasons why the Executive should not have that unlimited jurisdiction to suspend, which, if he has the right to suspend under the Constitution, he undoubtedly has.

"But why form a judgment, and then leave the whole judgment to the Executive as they must?" asks Mr. Binney. "Why claim for Congress the power to suspend, when the actual and efficient power as an Executive act, must be with the President? The Parliament of England delegates it to the Crown, because Parliament alone can surmount the Constitution, or restrict the operation of the Habeas Corpus Act, or declare an exception to it. Parliament must act; why must Congress act?"

In answer to these queries, we would ask, is it necessary to "leave the whole judgment" to the President? Cannot the Act suspending curtail his authority? Under the Constitution, has not the power having the right to suspend an unlimited power? Is not this very fact a reason that the power should be in Congress, so that they may place checks on the suspension, by a law? Is not Congress the deliberative body—the Executive the hand which executes their will? The Parliament delegates the right to detain, because the Parliament is the only power which can dispense with the laws; because it is the deliberative body; because it has seen the danger of allowing the King to dispense with laws, and suspend the privilege of the Writ, which he did by his Judges, by his orders, by his Privy Council, and his Court of Star Chamber, in times past. Has our Constitution within it the seeds of dissolution? Has it provided for its own destruction?

Congress occupies the position of Parliament, as far as its powers under the Constitution extend; it is the only power which can dispense with laws, abrogate them, suspend them. The Executive has no such power. We have seen the trouble the English people have had to obtain those privileges, which we have given up without a murmur.

As to the public safety, the right to watch over it belongs to no department of Government, but to all; it must necessarily rest with the whole power of the Government, Congress and the President, not Congress or the President separately; Congress suspend the privilege of the Writ, the President gives his sanction by approving the law, and exercising power under its authority. It is the King, Lords, and Commons suspend the effect of the Writ in England.

Mr. Binney grants (p. 33) that, 1st. "Neither the clause points directly to the power." 2d. "The power given to any of the departments does not point directly to the clause." That is, in the clause, no power is pointed out as the suspending—and singular to say, notwithstanding his argument that the Executive is the power having the care of the public safety,—that the power given to any of the departments does not point to the clause, the latter is very true; but if we grant that the power to watch over and take care of the public safety belongs to the Legislative and Executive powers united, which is the case, that power points directly to this clause; the power that is to watch over the public safety is the power to suspend. It is granted that there is nothing in either: how can the conclusion be that the effect of both is like a resultant in mechanics? It is difficult to comprehend how something can be the result of nothing. The definitions of a resultant in the books do not carry out the views of Mr. Binney.

7. *The Habeas Corpus clause in the Constitution requires a law to define it.*

To the objection that the clause in the Constitution requires a law to make it explicit; that if the power to act comes immediately, not mediately from it, it would be discretionary in the President, without limitation of time, Mr. Binney argues (p. 54) that such a law would be "an unnecessary form here. The *power carries a limitation of time with it.* It depends for its existence upon the existence of rebellion. The instant the rebellion is suppressed, the power is extinguished. *While rebellion lasts and the public safety is in danger*, the power is indispensable; and *the Constitution supplies it for the whole of that occasion.*"

This is all very true, if it is admitted that the President is the power who may suspend, deriving his power immediately from the Constitution. How long the suspension may continue, if he so gets his power, nobody can tell. How long he may deem the public safety to require the suspension, cannot be arrived at definitely. Where is the man ready to resign so formidable power, if he can constitutionally exercise it alone, is above it? The power may be indispensable during the continuance of a rebellion. That is no reason for Congress to be ousted of its right to judge, to deliberate on the subject. Cannot Congress tell when the rebellion is over as well—better—than the Executive? When it is necessary the suspension should expire, when to repeal the law, or to continue it?

"The position taken sometimes in regard to other provisions of the Constitution, that what a Constitution of government ordains generally, it means to be carried into effect by law, fails in a great variety of cases.

It fails, of course, when, what the Constitution ordains on a subject, *is all the law it requires; as where a power to perform an executive act is given*, and the Constitution by its own terms declares the effect of the act; *which is the case with suspension of the privilege of the Writ of Habeas Corpus.*" (B. p. 51.)

The proposition is, "that what a Constitution of Government ordains generally, it means to be carried into effect by law." A distinction must be here taken between what the Constitution ordains itself, and what it ordains generally, which requires a law to carry it into execution; for instance, the judicial power requires an Act of Congress to concur with the Constitution in conferring power on the Circuit Courts. (4 Dall. 8, 7 Cranch. 32, Ibid. 504, 3 Wheat. 336.) And the clause we are discussing ordains that, under certain contingencies, the Writ shall be suspended. This is express. But by whom are the contingencies to be asserted? By whom is the suspension to be made? For how long—where? This is general.

That which is fully expressed and set forth requires no law,—e. g., the powers vested in the Supreme Court by the Constitution. (7 Cranch. 32, 1 Kent. Com. 314.) If the opinion of C. J. Marshall, 4 Cranch. 93, is of any weight, "It," the Supreme Court, "disclaims all jurisdiction not given by the Constitution or the laws of the United States. Courts which are created by written law—i. e., the Constitution,—cannot transcend that jurisdiction; for the meaning of the term Habeas Corpus, resort may unquestionably be had to the Common Law; but the power to award the Writ by any of the courts of the United States, must be given by written law;" and he goes on to say that the Habeas Corpus clause required a law to bring it into life and activity.

This necessity of a law is soon disposed of by Mr. Binney, on the ground of English analogy, and that "the limitation in England is practically worth nothing. It is either *a show of supervi-*

sion without the reality, to please the discontented, or to disarm party opposition; or it is a manifestation of the superiority of Parliament to the Crown; *or it is the cantilena of Parliamentary jealousy of the Crown.* The ministers who pass it, can always renew it if they are in power; and if they are not, a perpetual Act would be repealed upon their downfall. There was not, it is believed, a single suspension Act in England, in the time of any of their rebellions, that was not renewed from session to session, until the rebellions were suppressed." (P. 54.)

This may be all so in England, but it does not follow that here we are to give our Executive unlimited power when he shall consider it to be for his or the Nation's interest, or that we should go back to Monarchy to preserve the Republic; to use the words of Sir Boyle Roche, in the Irish House of Commons, that we "should give up not merely a part, but the whole of the Constitution, to preserve the remainder." Members of Parliament are in for three years, and more influence may be exerted over them, than over our representatives; beside, the interest of the representative and constituent is more identical here than there: here he is taken from the people, there he is taken from men of old families, or the younger sons of the nobility. Beside this, if Parliament deem it unnecessary, it is very doubtful if the ministers in power can renew, or will attempt to renew. For instance, in one case (Statute 57 Geo. III.,) the Act was continued until 1st March, 1818, but was, on the 31st January, 1818, repealed; and if any one will take the trouble to read the Parliamentary Debates on the suspension of the effect of the Writ, he cannot but come to the conclusion, from the protests and speeches of the members, that it is, in England, a very difficult thing to suspend the operation of the Writ; beside, we have not ministers to continue it, neither is it likely that Parliament would dare to make such a perpetual Act; and as to renewed Acts continuing the old, they were, no doubt, very necessary—at least we are to presume so. That it is a manifestation of the power of Parliament over the Crown, is undoubted. The question is not so much the continuance of the suspension as the safest depositary of the power to suspend.

"What the objection requires," he remarks, "is an Act suspending the privilege from session to session, renewable as Congress shall see fit." (P. 54.)

This is not English analogy. The Parliament never suspend from session to session, but always to a limited time, because a meeting might not be called by the King for three years. It is a very strong objection to the exercise by the President of the power that there is no limitation. If, as it is thought has been proved, Congress is the power to suspend, where is the restriction on the Executive? He may suspend, in time of peace, whenever, wherever, or for whatever offence he may choose. It was said, in the

Message of the present Executive—extra session,—"Soon after the first call for militia, it was considered a duty to authorize the commanding General, in proper cases, *according to his discretion*, to suspend the privilege of the Writ of Habeas Corpus, or, in other words, *to arrest* and detain, without resort to the ordinary processes and forms of law, such individuals as *he might deem dangerous to the public safety.*" The effect of the Writ has been shown not to affect in any way a *legal* imprisonment. The effect of this suspension, according to the President, was to authorize the illegal arrest and detention of persons.

If Mr. Binney's argument is correct, the President may not only authorize arrests outside of Judicial process, but may detain persons who have committed no offence, at his pleasure. Suspension will "enable those who happen to have power, to imprison the citizen who has not been guilty of any offence, and subject him to just such rigor of confinement as their discretion, not *the law of the land*, may prescribe." We cannot, in this connexion, avoid quoting some remarks from the opinion of Derbigny, Justice, 1815, (3 Mart. La. Rep. 531,) delivered when the policy of Jackson, relating to the defence of New Orleans, was shown to have been efficient, and his popularity was at its height. "The Monarch who unites in his hands," said he, "all the powers, may delegate to his Generals an authority as unbounded as his own; but, in a Republic, where the Constitution has fixed the extent and limits of every branch, in time of war as well as of peace, there can exist nothing vague, uncertain or arbitrary in the exercise of any authority. The Constitution of the United States, in which everything necessary to the general and individual security, has been foreseen, does not provide that, in times of public danger, the Executive power shall reign to the exclusion of all others. It does not trust into the hands of a Dictator the reins of Government. The framers of that Charter were too well aware of the hazards to which they would have exposed the fate of the Republic by such a provision; and had they done it, the States would have rejected a Constitution stained with a clause so threatening to their liberties. In the meantime, conscious of the necessity of removing all impediments to the exercise of the Executive power, in cases of invasion or rebellion, they have permitted Congress to suspend the privilege of the Writ of Habeas Corpus if the public safety require it. Thus far goes the Constitution. Can it be asserted," remarks the same Judge, after an examination of the powers of Parliament, " whilst British subjects are thus secured against oppression in the worst times, American citizens are left at the mercy of the will of an individual who may, in certain cases—*the necessity of which is to be judged of by himself*—assume a supreme overbearing, unbounded power? The idea is not only repugnant to the principles of any free government, but subversive of the very foundations of our own." *Vide* opinion of

Kent, Judge of Supreme Court of New York, to same effect, in 1813. Case of In re Stacey, (10 Johnson Reports, 328,) which is somewhat similar to the case of Merryman.

8. *The Executive is the department most likely to abuse the power, and escape responsibility for such abuse.*

Mr. Binney remarks (p. 18:) "The suspension should obviously be with that department of the Government which is the least able of itself to abuse the power, and is the most easily and directly made amenable to responsibility and correction for abuse."

The questions arise under this, 1st. What department of the Government is least able of itself to abuse the power? 2d. What department is the most easily and directly made amenable to responsibility and correction for abuse?

Of the 1st—What department of Government is least able of itself to abuse the power? It needs no argument to convince the reader of history or the student of politics, that more security to the liberty of the citizen, or subject, may be found in the many than in one, in a Republic than in a Despotism. The many are less likely to use the power of arbitrary imprisonment than one;— there are counter influences among them, and each fears for himself; the one fears nobody, if that feeling is excepted which is in the breast of every autocrat—fear of the people as a mass. If correct in this argument, the Legislative is the proper power to suspend. It is the least able to abuse the power; because of the will of its constituents; because the representative goes into private life, subject to the laws he has made; because his wife, his children, his relations are subject; because his is not an arbitrary discretion— he is but one of many; because he is a man not of a particular State or section of country, having a control of the privilege, but one among men from different States, different sections, each in favor of the aggrandizement of his particular locality—this acting as a check upon each. For these reasons, a few among many that may be suggested, it results the Legislative is the proper power to suspend the privilege, but with the Executive as a component department.

2d. The most easily and directly made amenable to responsibility and abuse? Mr. Binney will hereafter argue from this proposition that the President, being amenable by impeachment, will not abuse his privilege; but he loses sight of a very important fact, that a President may, like "Mister Oliver Cromwell," come to the conclusion, that a Congress is incompatible with the public safety, and like that illustrious gentleman, abolish it altogether, or make it but a shadow—

"A schoolboy's tale, the wonder of an hour."

If so, how is he the most easily and directly amenable? Is he not Commander-in-chief of the army and of the navy, and is a People customarily careful of its rights in times of civil commotion? Does not history, when opened at the page which treats of the downfall of Republics, show that this is the method of obtaining power, the army, the navy, illegal arrests and languishing imprisonments? England, under the Long Parliament; France, under the Consulship of Napoleon; Italy, under the Cæsars.

Do not the times past point to those of the present as a warning for the future—to Greece, to Italy, to Venice, to England, and to France? We ask how can a President, if Mr. Binney's argument be correct, be the party most easily and directly made amenable to responsibility for abuse of the power of arbitrary imprisonment? But the most singular part of this elaborate argument of one of whom it can be justly said, "*multarum palmarum causidicus,*" is that in which it is argued that because the Executive is to take care that the laws be faithfully executed, and to defend and protect the Constitution as well as to support it; because there is nothing in the powers of his " office which could justly excite jealousy, or that he might abuse the suspending power," (B. p. 22;) because the Convention of 1787 showed the greatest jealousy in giving him powers; because they gave the power of impeachment to the House; because, unable to veto a law over a two-thirds majority—to make war, to arm a soldier, "*to call forth the militia for any purpose,*" or to make a treaty without the consent of the Senate, or appoint a porter in the post-office without the consent of Congress—unable to adjourn Congress unless both Houses do not agree as to the time; because, in short, "*the President has no powers that can be abused* or enlarged by himself, *except with more danger to himself than to the country;*" that therefore he is to have the power to imprison at his will, to detain a person imprisoned as long as he shall please—that that was the intention of the Convention of 1787—that every man, in case of the greatest tumult, the most unsettled state of the public mind, when the rebellion is caused by the opponents of a dominant party, flushed with victory, annoyed at recent conflict, and endeavoring to keep down that opposing party which it hates, and wishes to crush. Can it be presumed, does not the history of the past cause us to conclude, that the President, if he has the power to suspend this inestimable privilege, holds every man tenant at will of his liberty? We are men like those who are gone, subject to prejudices, to passions, to a domineering spirit. Are we not standing on the brink of a precipice, if Mr. Binney's argument is correct? Hope and Fear, Ambition and Prejudice, surround us in a crisis like that which is spoken of, and endeavor to hurl us onward to suit their purposes. Can it be presumed that a body composed of men like those which formed that Convention, could have intended to provide for despotism, for the destruction of the Government they were framing, to pave the way for a Monarch, to sow within their borders the seeds of disruption and anarchy?

The Convention deemed it wise to qualify the Common Law principle, remarks Mr. Binney, "*so as to protect the safety of the public in a season of great disorder*, and yet to prevent its defeat by any power in any other condition of the country." (P. 24.)

It was suggested in that Convention that this principle—that of immediate trial—should be adhered to without any exception, but it was thought better by the majority "to qualify and abridge the principle constitutionally, by annexing to it an exception most strictly limited to the occurrence of certain great and critical disturbances in the public condition of the country, and to let the public safety, at the times of such disturbance, and in those only, overrule the principle for the time and season."

This departure left the Writ under the exception in the same position as though nothing had been said in regard to it, the conditions before mentioned first occurring.

From these facts, and for these reasons, we arrive at the conclusion, that the Executive is most likely to abuse the power, and the most likely to escape responsibility for such abuses.

9. *The liability to Impeachment is not a sufficient check on the Executive to deter him from abusing the power of suspension, and is not a reason that he should have it.*

A very strong ground in favor of the right of the President, Mr. Binney says, arises from his liability to impeachment if he abuses the power of suspending the Writ, and being subject to this, he should have the power because the most directly amenable for the abuse of it. "Congress are irresponsible." He says, (p. 52) "Congress, in sympathy with the President by the grant, lessen the President's responsibility." This is not so; although not answerable to impeachment, they are answerable to their constituents and public opinion, a most powerful check in this country, for the necessity of the suspension, and the due exercise of the power; they lessen the President's responsibility for as much as they assume, and are so far responsible; the balance is vested in the Executive, subject to their law, and is under their control, subject to impeachment if abused. There is no part of the Constitution which requires an Act of Congress so much as this clause; an Act to define when suspension is to take place, for what and where. Congress are just as likely to be in sympathy with the President in case he suspends, and they can then shelter themselves under his wing, say they did not suspend to their constituents, escape responsibility themselves, and yet never impeach the Executive. Is not Congress likely to say, if the President has the discretionary right to suspend, you have done properly? Is not this opinion likely to come into being after detainer, after arrests, when the mischief is done? Is it not better to guard against an injury, than suffer by it and then guard against it? Must we submit to torture to know what the feeling is?

If the President has the power, he "directly and personally responsible for his own judgment and acts, makes the guarantee more complete than any other provision." (B. p. 52.)

Let us see whether the President can be impeached under the wording of this clause, is "directly and personally responsible for his own acts,"—it fixes nothing definite, no crimes for which suspension is to take place, no locality where it is to be, no time for which it is to last,—the important parts of the suspension are all to be ascertained by law; if Mr. Binney be correct, all these are matters of discretion resting with the Executive; we are to be governed in these matters by the arbitrary discretion of one man, who is also, according to him, to have the power of unlimited arrest, greater powers than has any Emperor of Europe. And the only checks for which it is claimed an impeachment of the Executive could occur, is in case the arrest and detainer was not, according to his discretion, for the purpose of putting down the rebellion; the only limitation on time, the existence of rebellion according to his opinion; the only limitation of locality, his will. (B. p. 41.) If he does wrong, he falls back on his patriotic intentions; (B. p. 52;) rather a feeble check, we think, for one vested with so much power.

Where is the responsibility for a matter of discretion? Mr. Binney thinks that the discretion cannot last longer than rebellion and the public safety may require detainer. How long may this be—for what offences must the arrests be made which justify detainer, and where? To whom is he responsible?. To Congress—for what? The wording of the Constitution is not sufficient to make him liable, except in cases of the grossest abuse, and nothing has been done, if Congress have not acted, for which he can be made liable to impeachment in other cases. If Mr. Binney be correct, we are tenants at will of our liberty. (B. p. 42.) It depends on the Executive's "reasonable ground of belief," which may be obtained from our personal enemies, from any spy, from any public informer; yet, according to him, " this is the Constitutional aspect of the suspension of the privilege of the Writ of Habeas Corpus, and of the public safety which is concerned in the exercise of the power." (Ibid.) It is certainly not the legal, or the legal-constitutional, if there be anything constitutional not legal.

Is not an ounce of prevention better than a pound of cure? A law should be made to prevent crime, by informing what is a crime, so that the Executive and others may know what is, or what is not to be done. Would it not be better for the Executive, if Congress said beforehand, you will not be held responsible for doing this, you may detain in these cases, thereby excluding other cases, and informing him of his responsibility in those other cases? Would it not be better for the people, and better for the Executive, that he or they may not rush blindly into an offence, without knowing that it is an offence, or that it subjects them to punishment? Further, suppose the Executive should be ambitious, should say as Cromwell did, The public safety requires the arrest of all the Legislative branch of the Government, would we not have a Despotism? How could he then be impeached? It is discretionary with him, having the power of unlimited arrest, unlimited detainer, the command of Army and Navy to submit to impeachment. That he is the weakest department—was made so by the Convention of 1787, is the doctrine of Mr. Binney. Should we disregard the doings of our ancestors—should we make him the strongest? Mr. Binney thinks, "as a theorem of republican polity, a most dangerous power, if this be most dangerous, should be lodged in the feeblest hands," so that that power, we surmise, may never become "the feeblest" again.

Some may say this would not be the case at the present time, the ruler is a good man, he is honest. The chances of the rulers always being good men, second Washington's or Cicero's, are rather Utopian. Let us not forget that the present is but the shadow of the past. We think the present better than that which is gone. Let us not forget that men have the same passions, prejudices, sin; that the present is as bad as the past; wars, crime, and self-interest, still are the faults of Nations.

"Show me that age and country where the rights and liberties of the people were placed on the sole chance of their rulers being good men, without a consequent loss of liberty," said Patrick Henry, in the Virginia Convention of 1788. "I say that the loss of that dearest privilege has ever followed, with absolute certainty, every such mad attempt." A principle bad in itself, should not be advocated on the probability that it may not be abused.

That men are governed by their interests, does not require a Rochefoucauld to convince us. "The man makes the motive, not the motive the man. What it is the man's interest to do or refrain from, depends less on any outward circumstances than on what sort of a man he is. If you wish to know what is practically a man's interest, you must know the cast of his habitual feelings and thoughts. Everybody has two kinds of interests, interests which he cares for, and interests which he does not care for. Everybody has selfish and unselfish interests; a selfish man has cultivated the habit of caring for the former, and not caring for the latter." (Mill on Govt. 123.) And more especially is this interest brought out when a man is in power. It is a universally observed fact, that a man prefers his selfish interests to those interests which he shares with others, and his immediate interests to those indirect or remote, and that these are especially called forth and fostered by the possession of power. The moment a man or class find themselves or itself with power in their or its hands, the individual interest, or the separate class interest, acquires an entirely new degree of importance in their eyes. Worshipped by others, they at last worship it themselves, and think themselves entitled to be counted at a hundred times the value of other people; *while the facility they ac-*

quire *of doing without regard to consequences, weakens gradually the habits which make men look forward even to those consequences which affect themselves.* This is the *rationale* of corruption by power, founded on universal tradition, history, and universal experience. (See J. S., Mill. on Govt. 124.) There is, to be sure, a certain amount of disinterestedness existing in the minds of all men, which is disguised by the name of patriotism, the interest of the few to be given up for that of the many, that of the many for the benefit of the Nation; this is, however, but interested disinterestedness, the consequences are for us, and for those who follow us, individually, or in the concrete.

The interest of the governing power is to control the people, the interest of the people is not to be controlled except when absolutely necessary for their benefit; in a doubtful case the people should have the advantage of the doubt—should have the power placed in the hands of those most identical in interest. It is the interest of the Government, that all its acts be pronounced correct and right, the interest of the people requires that those acts should be examined into and criticised, either by speech or writing; it is the interest of the Government to assume special privileges—to centralize,—the interest of the people requires that all should be on the same footing, as near as consistently may be, for the proper functions of the Government. The governing power is changing continually from centralization to an individuality of the people—from a Despotism to a Republic, and *vice versa.* In a Republic, the danger to be feared is, that the governing power will obtain more than its share; in a Despotism, that the people will. It is also an undoubted fact, that less is to be feared, in a Republic, from the deliberative body than the Executive—from the one that thinks, less than from the one that does. The power of impeachment is but a weak reed against an ambitious man, with the power of unlimited arrest and detainer.

The whole argument of Mr. Binney on this subject of impeachment, is founded on the premise that Congress would give the Executive the same unlimited power which he would have under the Constitution. "For the use of powers which Congress may give him, to be exercised *according to his own judgment,* it is only in flagitious cases of wanton oppression, that we can expect Congress to be his accuser, or the Senate his judges."

Whether Congress would give him powers "to be exercised on his own judgment," is very doubtful. It is not likely that Congress would invest him with the power of a Dictator; it is doubtful if they could,—beside, a Roman Dictator not absolute in power. He was only appointed for six months. There would, and certainly should be some restrictions on the discretionary power to detain, some offences, some time limited, some place specified, within whose borders an arrest is to justify detainer, some oath required, some notice given. For if he have the power of unlimited arrest and detainer

Constitutionally, is Commander-in-chief of the Army and Navy, and is enforcer of all laws of the United States, he has despotic power, and the powers of the Legislature, and the Judiciary, are but paper powers, to be annulled whenever he desires.

Absolute power is never given in England to the King; the power is given to the Privy Council and Secretaries of State, and they are liable to impeachment. There is, also, a saving of the privileges of the members of Parliament during its session, subject to its consent, to prevent, it is likely, the repetition of those scenes which disgraced the reign of the First Charles. The detention there is never for an indefinite period.

"There is in every Constitution a strongest power," says Mr. Mill,—"one which would gain the victory, if the compromises by which the Constitution habitually works itself, were suspended, and *there came a trial of strength.*"

Beside, Congress is not always in session to impeach, and acts might be done between the sessions of that body it might never sit to impeach. The power of impeachment would not be of the least avail to keep an ambitious man from seizing the reins of power. The office is short at the present time; but if Mr. Binney's argument is correct, the "short taper" might last for a lifetime, and many generations after. A curious assertion is made by Mr. Binney, (p. 54,) that "The exercise of the power would probably be continued *longer by renewable terms, from Congress to the President,* than the President of his own judgment would exercise it under the Constitution." The correctness of this we leave to the judgment of the reader; it needs no comment.

It must not be forgotten the past is a guide for the future, that the present must be the past to those who come after us, that the acts of long ago are looked at with veneration, and cited as authority, that the past should be the mirror of the present, into which we look for authority and direction, and that "We owe it to our ancestors to preserve entire those rights which they have delivered to our care; we owe it to posterity not to suffer their dearest inheritance to be destroyed;" (Junius, 201.)

The likelihood of the assertion quoted, is to be found in that which has just preceded. Goodness of the Executive must not be trusted; if it is to be, why have a Constitution? An ambitious President, on his own judgment, would not continue to exercise the power very long under the Constitution. The objection, which is called "technical," to the exercise, by the President, of the power on the ground "that it will stay the issuing of the Writ by the Federal Courts and Judges, or arrest proceedings under a Writ expressly authorized by Act of Congress," (p. 55,) which could only be stayed by a subsequent Act, is disposed of by Mr. Binney as English analogy: "The power of the President being derived from the Constitution, is above the authority of the Act." This assumes that the President has the power which, we think, has been shown to be fallacious. There can be no doubt of the fact that the suspension of the privilege of the Writ, either under the Acts relating to the Federal Courts, the State Constitutions, or the State Laws, is the suspension of laws.

If the President have the right under the clause in the Constitution, to use the words of Mr. Binney, (p. 52,) applied by him, if Congress has the power; "It is only in flagitious cases of wanton oppression, that we can expect Congress to be his accuser, or the Senate his judges. When his own judgment brings the power into exercise, and his own application of it works a wrong in any degree." These remarks show, it is thought, that the power of impeachment is not a sufficient check on the Executive.

10. *The decisions of the Courts, and the opinions of the text writers, are in favor of the assertion that Congress must join in the suspension.*

If the reader will consult the text books on the Constitution, he will find that they give the power to Congress. Mr. Binney has not cited one in his favor. The censure on the opinion of the Chief Justice of the United States, in the case of Merryman, June, 1861, on the ground of partiality, (B., p. 36,) is not just to one of the greatest jurists who ever adorned the Bench of this or any country, who is sworn to do his duty, and who presents as clean a record as any man; it does not advance Mr. Binney's argument in the least. We hope no one will be influenced by the remarks of Mr. Binney, and we also hope they were not inserted to prevent the free discussion of the subject.

Speaking of this opinion, we have the following singular assertion: "The remarkable feature of this opinion is, that for proof of the President's exclusion from the power, the Chief Justice dwells upon the President's brief term of office—his responsibility, by impeachment for malfeasance in office—the power of Congress to withhold appropriations for the Army, of which he is Commander-in-Chief, and to disband it if the President uses it for improper purposes—his limited power of appointment—his limited treaty-making power—his inability to appoint even inferior officers, unless he is authorized by Congress to do so. Chief Justice Taney has elaborately stated all this, without appearing to perceive that these very considerations *may have and* CERTAINLY OUGHT TO HAVE *induced the Convention to devolve upon* THE PRESIDENT EXCLUSIVELY, *the trust and power of suspending or not suspending the privilege in time of rebellion, as he should think the public safety required.* The constitutional limitations of the office make the President the safe and the safest depository of such a discretion. *There can be little danger of abuse from an office of such powers.* It was the great power of a King of England, that was the operative motive with Parliament for taking the power of suspension from him; and they have left it in a body that is of equal power under the Constitution, and apparently on its way to greater."

The latter part of this argument would apply with great force against the first part. Would not the Executive have as great power as the King of England ever had, if he could imprison and detain at pleasure? And is not the right to imprison of his own free will, whenever he shall deem it necessary for the public safety in times of rebellion, (which is said by Mr. Binney to be the effect of the suspension of the privilege,) and as long as he shall please, placing us in the position of freemen, holding our liberty at the pleasure of the Executive? Are we not going back to the days of William the First of England? Are we not annihilating with a stroke of the pen the labors of centuries, if we admit Mr. Binney to be correct? Can any one imagine, or assert in cool sober judgment, after reading the Debates in the Federal Convention, the determination shown to control the Executive in his powers; the negative given by all the delegates present, when it was proposed to give the Executive power to dispense with laws for a limited time; the evidences which Mr. Binney cites evinced by the present Constitution to cut down and control the power of the Executive. Can any one suppose from these facts—when the Constitution is silent; when the position of the clause was changed by the mover and the Committee on Style and Arrangement to its present position, under the head of restrictions on the powers of Congress; when English History and English Precedents pointed to the Legislative, as the proper party to dispense with the privilege of the Writ; when that History is but a repetition of repeated endeavors on the part of English Kings, to obtain the power from the English people, and of their resistance to such endeavors; when we see the whole of the Article under which Section 9th is to be found, is devoted to the Legislative branch of the Government, and not to the Executive; when not a word is said in relation to the subject in that Article, which confers power on the President; when there is a law of Congress on the Statute Book giving persons imprisoned a right to the Writ, which the Executive has no right to suspend; when it is inserted in the Constitution that Congress shall "have the power to make all laws which may be necessary and proper to carry into execution all powers vested by this Constitution in the Government of the United States, or in any department or officer thereof;" when no person is to "be deprived of life, liberty, or property, without due process of law"—that is, judicial process; when the sixth amendment provides that "in all criminal prosecutions, the accused shall enjoy the right to a speedy and public trial, by an impartial jury of the State and district wherein such crime shall have been committed, and be informed of the *nature* and cause of the accusation; to be confronted with the witnesses against him; to have compulsory process for obtaining witnesses in his favor; and to have the assistance of counsel for his defence;" when the Executive is to see that "the laws be faithfully executed;" when he is not authorized by the Constitution, to execute them himself or by means of his agents or officers; when the Government of the United States is known to be one of delegated and limited powers, that it derives its existence from the words of the Constitution only, and that the powers given are to be construed strictly, especially when in derogation of Common Right; when to make imprisonment lawful, it is an undoubted fact that it must be by process from the courts of judicature, by warrant from some legal authority to commit to prison, or when in a state of war, the arrest and detention by some military officer, of a belligerent or his emissary. Can we doubt for an instant, to use the words of Roger B. Taney, "If the President of the United States may suspend the Writ, then the Constitution of the United States has conferred upon him more *regal* and *absolute* power over the liberty of the citizen, than the people of England have thought it safe to intrust the Crown; a power the Queen of England cannot exercise at this day, and which could not have been lawfully exercised by the sovereign, even in the reign of Charles the First."

Mr. Binney comments upon the case of the *Ex parte* Bolman, 4 Cranch. p. 75, cited by Justice Taney as follows, (we shall make some few alterations which the reported case justify:)

"But the language of Chief Justice Marshall, whatever be its meaning, was not used in a case which brought up the question. The case of *Ex parte Bolman* in 4 Cranch, could not bring up the question whether the President or Congress had the power of suspending the privilege of the Writ in cases of rebellion or invasion. There was no rebellion nor invasion at the time; and no suspension of the privilege by either Congress or the President."

That there was a rebellion, will be shown in treating of the attempt at suspension in 1807.

"The question before the Court, the first in *Ex parte* Bolman, was whether the Supreme Court, having no original jurisdiction of the case, could issue a Writ of Habeas Corpus to bring up the body of Bolman, and " (a writ of certiorari to bring up) "the record of his commitment by the Circuit Court of the District of Columbia. The Court was somewhat divided upon the point, and the Writ was issued, two judges out of the five dissenting." (But one dissented, he stating that his opinion was supported by that of one of his brethren, who was by sickness rendered unable to attend.) "But the manner in which it was argued, not at all the necessities of the case, induced the Chief Justice to say, 'that if at any time the public safety should require the suspension of the powers (i. e., of issuing Writs of Habeas Corpus) vested by this Act (the Judiciary Act of 1789,) in the Courts of the United States, it is for the Legislature to say so. That question depends upon political considerations, on which the Legislature are (is) to decide. Until the Legislative will be expressed, this Court can only see its duty, and must obey the laws."

"The Legislature had given this power to the Court," to issue the Writ, remarks Mr. Binney, "it is apparently reasonable to say, that the Legislature only could suspend that power."

This, together with what has been cited, shows the opinion so clearly, it is impossible any one can doubt it. The Legislature have given the power to the court, the Legislature must, therefore, suspend. Mr. Binney must grant that the suspension by the President is of the power of this court, if he has the power to suspend; and that the opinion of the Chief Justice, relating to the suspension, although but a dictum, is nevertheless the opinion of a learned lawyer, and, as such, is entitled to some weight.

Indeed, he goes on to say, "the whole language does, however, say farther, that if the *public safety* should require *the suspension of the powers vested in the courts, adverting, perhaps*, to the language of the Habeas Corpus clause in the Constitution, it was for the Legislature to say so." (B. p. 38.)

It is undoubted that the power that makes the law, is the power to suspend it; more especially would this be so under our Constitution, if we but remember that a vote was taken, in the Convention which framed it, on giving the President the power to suspend, and that it was negatived by all the States.

Is not a suspension of the privilege a suspension of one of the powers vested in the courts? Is it necessary to take away all the powers at once? Does it not amount to the same, if taken away by the President, one by one? Must not the same power do this, that can suspend *in toto?*

"But there was nothing before the Chief Justice to raise the distinction, between *the privilege of the Writ as descriptive of a personal right*, and the *Writ itself as authorized by law;* nor between the operation of the Constitution itself, and the operation of a law of Congress." (B. p. 38.)

True; yet we must not forget that the subtle distinction between the personal Privilege and the Writ, between the operation of the Constitution and the law of Congress, as claimed by Mr. Binney, had not been broached at that time; and we must not forget that the Judge said, that if the law had not been passed, there would have been no privilege in the court; "if the means be not in existence, the privilege itself would be lost, although no law for its suspension should be enacted." This question was certainly *res judicata.*

The strictures upon the remarks of Judge Story, (B. p. 39,) are true. He does take for granted that Congress is the proper power to suspend the Writ, or the privilege of it. He states it as undoubted law; and when we think of his great reputation as a constitutional jurist, this statement should have some weight.

We would also refer to another Commentator, our fellow-townsman, William Rawle, Esq.:—

"This Writ is believed to be known," he says, "only in countries governed by the Common Law, as it is established in England; but in that country the benefit of it may at any time be withheld by the authority of Parliament, whereas we see in this country it cannot be suspended, even in cases of rebellion or invasion, unless the public safety shall require it. Of this necessity the Constitution probably intends that the Legislature of the United States shall be the judges. Charged as they are with the preservation of the United States from both these evils, and superseding the powers of the several States, in the prosecution of the several measures, they may find it expedient to adopt, it seems not unreasonable that this control over the writ of *habeas corpus*, which ought only to be exercised on extraordinary occasions, should rest with them. *It is, at any rate, certain that Congress, which has authorized the courts and judges of the United States to issue writs of Habeas Corpus, in cases within their jurisdiction, can alone suspend their power.*" (Rawle on Cons., 118.)

"Congress, under the Constitution," Mr. Binney thinks, (p. 39,) "might adopt any form of judicial relief, and endow its judicial department accordingly—the civil law process, "*de homino libero exhibendo*," or the Spanish "*el despacho de manifestacion.*" If Congress had taken either, it would not have altered in the least the effect of the clause in the Constitution."

But if Congress had done so, according to Judge Marshall, a Writ of Habeas Corpus could not have been issued out of the United States Courts. He says Congress had to provide the means, (4 Cranch. 95;) when they did so, the clause went into effect as far as the power of the Federal courts was concerned. It went into effect with the Constitution, as far as the State constitutions, laws, and courts were concerned. If Mr. Binney be correct, the clause in the Constitution applying to the former courts, would not be of any effect. Congress could suspend the Spanish process, or the procedure under the Corpus Juris Civile, if they had been adopted, whenever it pleased. It is doubtful whether this can be done, as to the privilege of the Writ of Habeas Corpus: if it can, great injustice might be done, by means of arrests by the process of the Federal courts, to which State process would not apply, unless it be granted the Constitution, by guarantying, gives the Writ.

Mr. Binney, in order to overcome the plain intent and meaning of the clause, which he says is technical, (p. 9,) gives as the reason for its use, that it means the privilege of relief from imprisonment by bail, &c., and that "the writ of Habeas Corpus was better known in the States, and therefore most appropriate; but the privilege is not inseparably bound to that or any other specific remedy. *The reference to the writ was to describe the privilege intelligibly, not to bind it to a certain form.*" (B., p. 40.)

This is not so, according to his remarks, (p. 9.) The reference is to a known legal writ, the effect of which Mr. Binney confounds with the Writ. The clause does not refer to any writ, but to a certain known writ, having a scientific meaning; it is the privilege of this legal writ, which is not to be suspended, not that of any writ Congress may authorize to issue—not of the writ of Summons or *Capias ad respondendum.* The Convention used technical words; and when words of Art are used, we are bound to presume they were used in their known and usual meaning and signification.

The case of Martin vs. Mott,—12 Wheaton, 19,—is cited as an authority governing the case of rebellion, (B. p. 44;) this is not so. The case of Mott arose from his not obeying a call of the President for militia to repel invasion; Mott not obeying was fined, his goods being seized for the payment, he replevied them, upon which an avowry was filed; judgment was entered in the State Court for Mott; the case was then brought to the Supreme Court of the United States. The clause of the Act of 1795, referring to the case of invasion, says, "that it shall be lawful for the President to call forth such number of the Militia *as he may judge necessary* to repel such invasion, and to issue orders for that purpose to such officers as he may think proper; and in case of insurrection in any State, against the *Government thereof,* on application of the Governor, when the Legislature cannot be convened, or of the Legislature, to call forth the Militia of the other States to suppress the same," (*vide,* Cons., Sec. 4, Art. IV.,) and then we have the section mentioned by Mr. Binney, (B. p. 44.) This we have given (Ante, p. 66) The wording of this section is very different from that of the first. The case in 12 Wheaton was under the 1st section. By it the President is to judge of the fact,—Congress have given him the power so to judge, and if necessary, to call forth the Militia. By the second, the President is not to judge in the first instance; in both cases he is acting under the law of Congress—the discretion comes from them. The power confided by Congress to the President, says Justice Story, in the above mentioned case, "is doubtless of a very high and delicate nature,"—this was as to the first section, the only one before the Court. "It is, in its terms, a limited power, confined to cases of *actual invasion,* or imminent danger of invasion. Is the President the sole and exclusive judge whether the exigency has arisen—or is it to be considered as an open question, upon which every officer to whom the orders of the President are addressed may decide himself—and equally open to be contested by every Militia-man who shall refuse to obey the orders of the President? We are all of opinion, that the authority to decide whether the exigency has arisen, belongs exclusively to the President, and that his decision is conclusive upon all other persons,"—this refers only to the 1st section. "We think," said the Judge, "this construction necessarily *results from the nature of the power itself, and from the manifest object contemplated by Congress.*" (Ibid.)

From this case, the conclusion is arrived at, that the judgment of the President on the facts is conclusive on everybody.

"The President, from the very nature of the facts, and the duty of his office, decides them himself. He decides the fact of rebellion. He declares the number of militia necessary to cope with the insurrection." (B. p. 44.)

From this case, and the fact that it is for the Executive to see that the laws be faithfully executed, and that he is to know officially that the execution of the law is obstructed by powerful combinations, and that the Marshal's power is futile, is derived the President's power to dispense with, and abrogate the Acts of 1789, 1833 and 1842, and all of the Bills of Rights, Constitutions and Statutes of the States, conflicting with that which he deems his authority, when if he has the right to dispense with the Writ, under the clause in the Constitution, he has the right supreme and untrammelled. From this case, and these facts, it is deduced that "it is manifest then that there is no necessity for a *law* of Congress to determine the great fact of rebellion or invasion, or the general or particular danger to the public arising from it, upon which the suspension of the privilege of the Writ depends," that—"from the dawn of the Government, *Congress has left these facts with the President, and with him alone.*" (B. p. 44.)

The case of Luther vs. Borden,—7 Howard Rep., 1,—(B. p. 55,) is rather against Mr. Binney's opinion. "The Writ of Habeas Corpus," says Judge Woodbury, page 48, in a very learned dissenting opinion on the subject of Martial Law, "unless specially suspended by the Legislature having power to do so, is as much in force in intestine war as in peace."

In considering this case, it must not be forgotten, that the Legislatures of the States have all the rights not prohibited to them; and the right to declare Martial Law does not appear to have been prohibited to the Legislature of Rhode Island by the Charter. The Constitution of the United States differs from that of the States, as to the powers under it, as has been shown. The State Government of Rhode Island, under the old Charter, had, very likely, the right to order arrests without warrant, or declare Martial Law; this is not the case under the Constitution of the Union.

Mr. Binney refers (p. 53) to the action of the Senate, 1807, after the reception of the message of President Jefferson, relative to the conspiracy of Aaron Burr; in support of his argument, that greater danger to the liberties of the people would exist if Congress must join in the suspension, than if exercised by the Executive alone. He says, "There was neither invasion nor insurrection in its lowest stage;" that Mr. Jefferson favored the theory, that Congress alone had the power to suspend, and sent a message to Congress so "that he might safely exercise it under their wing;"—"then followed the phenomenon, we might say the portent:" says he, "a Senate representing free States, under the Constitution, passed, within closed doors," (the Senate, for several years after the formation of the present Government, sat with closed doors;) "a bill suspending the *privilege* of the Writ for three months, as to any and *all persons charged* on *oath* with treason, &c., endangering the peace, safety, or neutrality of the United States, and arrested by the warrant of the President, or by any one acting under his direction or authority." There was nothing like rebellion or invasion in the land.

"We are officially informed," said Mr. Elliott in the Congress of 1807, "that rebellion has reared its hydra front in the peaceful valleys of the West." (An. of 9th Congress, 2d Session, 407, &c., q. v.) The militia of Ohio, Kentucky, Tennessee, Mississippi and Orleans territory, and one thousand regular troops, were ordered out to quell it. As to Mr. Jefferson, we should not forget, that in 1787, he objected to the Constitution because it did not provide "for the eternal and unremitting force of the Habeas Corpus laws." In 1788 he advised four States should refuse to ratify it until a Declaration of Rights was annexed to it, asserting that there should be "no suspension of the Habeas Corpus."

"Happily," says Mr. Binney, "there was virtue enough in the House of Representatives, or *enough of* ALIENATION FROM MR. JEFFERSON, to make the House reject the bill by an immense majority, and to open their doors. But we may ask, with all confidence, whether Mr. Jefferson, even with a consciousness of his own power under the Constitution to suspend the privilege, would have executed such a purpose, at such a time, upon his own responsibility? We may confidently say *no*. But if a majority of the House had acquiesced, and there were nineteen who voted for it, we may recollect whose sentiment it was, upon being told that his friends were willing to ignore a breach of the Constitution, which he had expressly acknowledged, replied, that '*if his friends were satisfied, he would acquiesce with satisfaction.*' This getting power from friends in Congress who *are satisfied*, is a prodigious corroborative in the exercise of it, whether it be Constitutional or not."

But this statement is neither just to Mr. Jefferson, nor entirely warranted by the facts. The latter remark was made upon another occasion, relating, we believe, to the purchase of Louisiana in 1803. The vote in Congress was strongly in favor of the purchase. Mr. Jefferson was not altogether in favor of it on Constitutional grounds, although it has been since considered one of the greatest events of his Administration. He proposed an *ex post facto* amendment to the Constitution to sanction it. His message certainly does not warrant the assertion that he wished the privilege suspended. "It will be seen," said he, "that of three of the principal emissaries of Mr. Burr, whom the General had caused to be apprehended, one had been liberated by Habeas Corpus, and the two others, being those particularly employed in the endeavor to corrupt the General and Army of the United States, have been embarked by him for our ports in the Atlantic States; probably on the consideration that an impartial trial could not be expected during the present agitations of New Orleans, and that that city was not as yet a safe place of confinement. As soon as these persons shall arrive, *they will be delivered to the custody of the law, and left to such course of trial, both as to place and process, as its functionaries may direct.*" (See also special message; An. 9th Congress, 2d Session, p. 45.) These men were Dr. Bolman and Swartwout. (Mentioned 4 Cranch. 75.)

The proceedings in the Senate, January 23d, 1807, the day after receiving the message referred to, were very singular. On motion of Mr. Giles, he, with two others, was appointed a committee to inquire whether it was expedient, in the then "state of public affairs, to suspend the privilege of the Writ of Habeas Corpus," and the message and documents received from the President, were referred to the committee, whereupon Mr. Giles reported a bill to suspend the privilege of the Writ, viz. :—

"That in all cases, where any person or persons, charged on *oath* with treason, misprision of treason, or other high crime or misdemeanor, endangering the peace, safety, or neutrality of the United States, have been or shall be arrested or imprisoned, by virtue of any warrant or authority of the President of the United States, or from the Chief Executive Magistrate of any State or Territorial Government, or from any person acting under the direction or authority of the President of the United States, the privilege of the writ of habeas corpus shall be, and the same hereby is suspended, for and during the term of *three months* from and after the passage of this act, and no longer."

The committee also reported a message to accompany the bill to the Representatives. (An. 9th Congress, 2d Session, p. 44.)

January 26th, 1807, the House of Representatives received the message from the Senate, and the bill. The House having been first cleared to receive them, it was then moved that the doors be opened, and the message should not be kept secret. Yeas, 123; nays, 3. (Ibid, 402.)

Mr. Eppes (Mr. Jefferson's son-in-law,) moved that the bill be rejected, which was afterwards withdrawn with the intent to renew it. "The President holds out the idea," said one member, "that the correct and proper mode of proceeding can be had under the existing laws. This was not the first instance; there had been two insurrections, both of which defied the authority of Congress, and had menaced the Union with dissolution. One justified the calling out of fifteen thousand men, and the expenditure of one million of dollars, yet he had not heard of any proposition to suspend the writ of habeas corpus." (Ibid, 404.) "Have we a right," said another, "to suspend it in any and every case of invasion and rebellion? So far from it, we are under a Constitutional interdiction not to act, unless the existing rebellion threatens the first principles of the national compact, and the Constitution. The Executive assures us that the public safety is not endangered. Can we, under these circumstances, consent to the investiture of that department with dictatorial powers? It would be contrary to the spirit of the Constitution." (Ibid, 407.) "It is in a free country," said Mr. Eppes, "the most tremendous power which can be placed in the hands of a *legislative body*. It suspends the chartered rights of the community, and places even those who pass the act, under military despotism." (Ibid, 409.) The bill was rejected on the first reading. Yeas, 113; nays, 19. (Ibid, 424.) All Mr. Jefferson's supporters but two, it is believed, voted for rejection. (Ibid, 416–423, Rand. Life of Jefferson, Vol. 2, p. 196.) The majority of the House were, at this time, in his favor, but twenty-seven were Federalists. (Jeff. Works, Letter February 27th, 1807, Vol. 5, p. 48.) The Federalists took Burr's case as their own. We do not find anything in Jefferson's Works or correspondence, of the period when this occurred, in favor of or against it. How it can be asserted that Mr. Jefferson was in favor of the suspension, it is difficult to understand.

There is also cited, by Mr. Binney, (B. p. 49,) a portion of No. 74 of the Federalist, which has especial reference to the pardoning power of the Executive. The wording of Clause 2, Sec. II. of Art. II., is: "The *president* shall have power to grant reprieves and pardons for offences," &c. There is a person, a power, designated who is to do this—"the President." The argument of Mr. Hamilton is: "If it should be observed," (that is, by those in opposition to having the clause in the Constitution,) "that a discretionary power, with a view to such contingencies, may occasionally be conferred upon the President," (that is, by the Legislature,) "it may be answered," by those in favor of the insertion of the clause, "whether, in a limited Constitution, that power could be *delegated by law*," or, in other words, whether the Constitution is not to be construed strictly, whether that—i. e., the power to pardon—might not be a power beyond the scope of Congress to confer on the President, whether, in short, any body could pardon, in the cases mentioned in the clause, if no power was given to the President by the Constitution; if the clause had read that such offences could be pardoned as are therein mentioned. In such a case could the power to pardon be delegated by Congress to the President? This is thought by Mr Binney to be "applicable to the power of arrest and detention in time of rebellion, as it is to the power of pardon."

It appears to be directly against him; the power he is claiming is a discretionary power, of more vital importance than that of pardoning. The Habeas Corpus clause is the most important for liberty of the citizen in the Constitution. By it no power is given to the President; a discretionary power exists as to the detainer;

what the public safety requires during a rebellion, who is to be detained, and for what, and where, are matters of opinion—discretion. No class of offences are mentioned in the Constitution, no place where the suspension is to take place; yet, against history, facts, law, analogy to the custom of the Government from which was obtained Privilege, Writ, and Suspension,—against the fact that it is doubtful whether Congress can give such discretionary power; and that that was the view of Mr. Hamilton, a member of the Convention of 1789, and that such power would have been given to the President in the Constitution, if he had been the power to exercise that discretion, outside of, and free from, the control of the deliberative branch,—the branch to think,—to have discretion, if any be needed. If such had been the intent of that Convention, when all these facts are considered, does the quotation from the Federalist advance the views of Mr. Binney? Is it not an authority to show, that Congress was intended to be a component power in case a suspension of the privilege of the Writ be necessary?

"It is also said, that the exercise of the power by the President, without oath or descriptive warrant, violates one of the amendments to the Constitution. It would be the same if the power were exercised by Congress." (B. p. 55.)

This is true; Congress have, under the Constitution, no right to arrest or detain in this way. The Constitution is explicit—no person can "be deprived of liberty without due process of law;"— the oath must be made, the warrant must be founded on probable cause, and the same rules apply to the Executive. The power is to authorize the suspension of the privilege of the Writ, the right to ask for an examination into the commitment, which will necessarily prevent bail, trial or discharge. This is the farthest any or all the departments can go outside of the courts of justice. They cannot pass a *privilegium*. According to Mr. Binney, we have no right to presume that the President will not require an oath. Are we to wait until we see if a dagger be sharp before we ward it off? Are we to try the experiment, whether a President will injure or not, and give him the power to do so, that this valuable fact may be ascertained?—experience first, avoid afterwards.

"If the amendment applies, he must do it, (that is, require the oath,) or the commitment will be irregular." (B. p. 55.)

Who is to say that the commitment is irregular? According to the argument on the other side, the Executive would be the power.

"Either the language of the amendment, though general, speaks in reference to the normal condition of the country only, when there is no rebellion or invasion and consequent war, foreign or civil." (Ibid.) Or it does not, "under such circumstances," (i. e., if it does not speak of the normal condition; when there is no rebellion,) "the rebellion or invasion supersedes the amendment for the time. The former seems to be the preferable conclusion;" (Ibid.;) therefore the rebellion or invasion does not supersede the amendment. Whether this is the meaning intended, we do not know. The paragraph seems to imply, Mr. Binney intended that the abnormal condition of the country would supersede the amendment. The argument, as stated, does not arrive at this conclusion; nor would it on the facts, if stated logically.

Another very subtle argument is, that "discretionary imprisonment is an arbitrary ouster from all the benefits of government, benefits which belong to every citizen, until he is accused and convicted of a crime;" therefore, the Legislature have no natural title to it, the word natural is here used by Mr. Binney, in a different sense from that used by those, who think "that to attribute to the President a power of suspending the privilege, is to deprive the Legislature of a power which *naturally* belongs to that body." (B., p. 56.) The word *naturally* is here used to signify, that which should belong to that body according to the usual course of things, a person would say, that right naturally should belong to me, it is used by this person in the sense of regularly, ordinarily, or conformably to the usual course of things. Mr. Binney puts another construction upon the word, using it in the sense of natural as applied to innate feelings, or to natural law, he virtually says in a state of nature, the right to be free, to do just as you please should be guarantied, discretionary imprisonment, no matter how necessary, is an ouster of all the benefits of Government; true, it is an ouster of the benefits of Government, but if done *lawfully* it is an ouster for the benefit of the whole, if for the benefit of the whole, if it is our natural liberty so far restrained and no farther than is for the good of all, of the community, and no one has a right to complain. It is not meant by these remarks to imply, that the Legislature has any rights beyond those in the Constitution.

If nothing had been said in the Constitution, Congress could have dispensed with the Writ undoubtedly, as far as the United States courts were concerned. It would still have been a violation of the natural rights of the individual if arrested. It is now *an ouster of all benefits* of Government, shortly before Mr. Binney thought the right of exemption from imprisonment, except by the law of the land, was not suitable for modern times. (B., p. 13—18.)

It is now thought by Mr. Binney "if the Constitution had not ordained the exception, no department of the Government could have enforced it, without violating the fundamental principle of every free Government." (B. p. 56.) Discretionary imprisonment is still the theme; it is not acknowledged that the Constitution has ordained an exception as to it, say that it did, would it not, as far as the exception is concerned, violate the natural rights of individuals, granting Mr. Binney's argument as correct? Is it not, under the exception a violation, if he is correct, even if by the President?

From all this, the conclusion is arrived at, that "it" (it is not known whether the discretionary right to arrest, or to suspend, or both are intended by this pronoun, both will be presumed) "can only be enforced now, by that department of Government, which can alone execute the ordinances of the Constitution, that are executive in their character, unless some other department be expressly named." (Ibid.)

The right of arrest *ad libitum* cannot be enforced by any department, according to any law or construction of the Constitution, the right to enforce the performance of the suspension must rest with the Executive; it does not follow from this, that he is the power to suspend or to arrest, nor does it require an express naming of another power to oust him; construction, contemporaneous exposition and history are sufficient. The objection that the Legislature is the power, Mr. Binney thinks is "one of those evils which the Executive department is exposed to, from the predominance of the legislative power under every Democratic Constitututtion." (Ibid.)

It certainly does not follow, that "at such seasons it is of less importance in what branch of the government the power of applying the limitation is vested." (B., p. 18.) It is of the most vital importance in times of rebellion or invasion, in what part of the Government the power of applying the limitation is vested. It is the only time the power is called into exercise, rebellions usually arise from some abuse by the governing power. Far be it from us to assert that this rebellion has so arisen; but people are not usually disposed to change the form of their Government, for every whimsy of the mind or fancy of the brain; arrests are then frequent, and most frequently upon suspicion; men's minds are tainted with suspicion, prejudice, and a desire to make every one conform to their own views; informers abound, who seek to benefit themselves by injuring others, perhaps, men they dislike; liberty is hanging down in the balance, and it requires a wise statesman to equalize men's minds, to make life worth having, to prevent anarchy, to avoid confusion. How a gentleman of the abilities of Mr. Binney can advance as a fact the proposition we have just quoted, we cannot understand, unless he has lately become a disciple of the Philosopher of Malmsbury.

In conclusion, we have shown that the normal condition of the English, and we their descendants, is freedom, subject to the law; that it was against encroachments upon their liberty, our ancestors have been contending for centuries; that the President has not and should not have the right to arrest outside of the courts of justice; that the word "privilege" in the clause in the Constitution we have been discussing, means the right of citizens of this country to ask for the Writ of Habeas Corpus, a Writ known only to us and our ancestors, a right to a legal Writ; that it was not intended to have the meaning Mr. Binney has ascribed to it; that his argument applies to the effect, not the privilege of the Writ; that the English custom is to deny the effect to a day certain—the suspension under the Constitution is to be of the privilege; that the great contentions in England have been really, whether the King could arrest, or suspend the Writ, by illegal warrants, courts, and Judges holding office at his pleasure; that at last, Parliament, representing the people, was victorious; that, since 1690, the power of suspension has been exercised by Parliament; that the ministers did previously that which Mr. Binney contends is correct, and Parliament indemnified, did not impeach them, as he thinks Congress would do if the President acted unpatriotically; that the power has been since exercised by Parliament, without any difficulty with the people. These facts, and the Acts of the members of the Convention of 1787, and the State conventions, together with the views of cotemporaneous statesmen, lawyers, politicians and the people, with the wording and intent of the Constitution derived from the instrument, show that it was intended for all time, for war as well as peace; that the power of dispensing with other parts of the Constitution, and statutes made under it, with State constitutions, Bills of Rights, statutes, the Common Law and customs, in short, suspending the privilege of the Writ, should be in Congress and the Executive, not in either alone; unless we except the case of the passage of an Act over the President's veto, in which case he is to carry out their wishes. The one to deliberate, the other to act; the one to say what is to be done, the other to do.

And now, reader, it is for thee to judge, whether the writer has succeeded in making the bud Reason expand sufficiently to thy sight, so that thou canst see the corolla of the flower Judgment, or whether the petals be crumpled and crisped, and the corol hidden; whether he has supported it with the stem of Truth and the leaves of Justice; and whether History and Law, the soil in which he has planted it, be ploughed or fallow; that he has watered it with Labor, he will not gainsay: but the plant has been short in arriving at its present state, and is, therefore, not perfect. His hope, however, is that his feeble endeavor may, to use the quaint illustration of Sir Francis Bacon, "awaken better spirits, like a bell ringer which is first up, to call others to church," and will incite some learned man to devote his energies to its further development, when, by his labor and the revivifying rays of the glorious sun of Liberty, we may see the clouds which now environ us disappear, the plant arrive at maturity, and this dangerous heresy averted from our land.

February 12th, 1862.

www.ingramcontent.com/pod-product-compliance
Lightning Source LLC
Chambersburg PA
CBHW031120160426
43192CB00008B/1059